THE CATHOLIC BIBLICAL QUARTERLY MONOGRAPH SERIES

12

TEMPLE PROPAGANDA:
THE PURPOSE AND CHARACTER OF 2 MACCABEES

by

Robert Doran

TEMPLE PROPAGANDA:
THE PURPOSE AND CHARACTER OF 2 MACCABEES

By

Robert Doran

The Catholic Biblical Association of America
Washington, DC 20064
1981

TEMPLE PROPAGANDA:
THE PURPOSE AND CHARACTER OF 2 MACCABEES
By Robert Doran

© 1981 The Catholic Biblical Association of America
Washington, DC 20064

PRODUCED IN THE UNITED STATES

Library of Congress Cataloging in Publication Data

Doran, Robert, 1940-
  Temple propaganda.

  (Catholic Biblical quarterly: Monograph series; 12)
  Bibliography: p.
  Includes index.
  1. Bible. O.T. Apocrypha. Maccabees, 2nd—Criticism, interpretation, etc.
I. Title. II. Series.
BS1825.2.D67   299'.73   81-10084
ISBN 0-915170-11-6   AACR2

TABLE OF CONTENTS

ABBREVIATIONS

In addition to the abbreviations listed in Instructions to Contributors to the *CBQ* and the CBQMS, the following abbreviations and sigla are used.

FGH   Jacoby, F. *Die Fragmente der griechischen Historiker.* Leiden: Brill, 1954-64.

The abbreviations for classical authors will be the same as those used in LSJ (rev. ed. with supplement; Oxford: Clarendon, 1968) xvi-xxxviii.

Unless otherwise noted, I have used as translations the *Revised Standard Version* of the Bible; Edgar J. Goodspeed, *The Apocrypha* (New York: Vintage, 1959), except for 1 Maccabees where I have used J. Goldstein, *1 Maccabees* (AB 41; Garden City, NY: Doubleday, 1976); and, where it exists, the LCL.

ACKNOWLEDGMENTS

I wish to thank in particular John Strugnell of Harvard Divinity School for his patient persistence in listening to my ideas and reading my drafts. Vir sapiens et humilis. The wide learning of Albert Henrichs of Harvard's Classics Department also was of great help. Amherst College generously helped towards typing the manuscript.

My greatest debt, however, is to my wife, Susan Niditch—not only for her joy, but also for her knowledge of the Bible and her literary sensitivity.

INTRODUCTION

2 Maccabees has never achieved popularity among scholars. One would have thought that it had much in its favor. As one of the few works written in Greek from the 2nd-1st cent. B.C.E. that have survived, it merited some attention. However, few classicists writing on historiography refer to it. Its second chance at success lay in its account of a short, but important, phase of Jewish history. Alas, here it was upstaged by the apparently more reliable, because more sober, account of 1 Maccabees: historians, except for B. Niese,[1] disparaged the work of 2 Maccabees.

Recently, it has come somewhat more into favor. The historical order of 2 Maccabees, where Antiochus IV dies before the purification of the temple, has been vindicated by the discovery of the list of Seleucid kings.[2] Such a vindication showed the order of 1 Maccabees to be incorrect. Even after this, however, no thorough literary analysis of 2 Maccabees has been made. In fact, there never has been a complete literary analysis of 2 Maccabees. The analyses that have been offered have appeared as part of introductions to commentaries on the work. The history of scholarship on 2 Maccabees, in fact, reveals that the viewpoints of two men have had the greatest influence on the literary judgment of the work: the best philological commentary remains the 1857 work of C. L. W. Grimm;[3] B. Niese's thesis that 2 Maccabees belongs to the genre of pathetic or rhetorical historiography, first enunciated in 1900,[4] has not been seriously challenged, even though the existence of such a genre is in serious question. A literary analysis is long overdue.

Two recent studies claimed that they would provide such an analysis. However, the literary interest of J. G. Bunge is primarily on the level of

---

[1] B. Niese, "Kritik der beiden Makkabäerbücher nebst Beiträgen zur Geschichte der makkabäischen Erhebung," *Hermes* 35 (1900) 268-307; 453-527. Published in book form as *Kritik der beiden Makkabäerbuch* (Berlin: Weidmann, 1900).

[2] A. J. Sachs and D. J. Wiseman, "A Babylonian King List of the Hellenistic Period," *Iraq* 16 (1954) 202-211; J. Schaumberger, "Die neue Seleukiden-Liste BM 35603 und die makkabäische Chronologie," *Bib* 35 (1955) 423-435.

[3] C. L. W. Grimm, *Zweites Buch der Maccabäer* (Kurzgefasstes exegetisches Handbuch zu den Apokryphen des Alten Testamentes; Leipzig: S. Hirzel, 1857).

[4] See footnote 1.

source criticism.[5] His overall thrust remains the reconstruction of the historical events of the Maccabean uprising. In contrast, the thesis of W. Richnow
abstracts completely from such historical reconstruction.[6] Richnow lays
stress on the rhetorical techniques and style of the author of 2 Maccabees,[7]
but he can hardly claim to have made a thorough literary analysis. Richnow
leaves out of discussion the letters prefixed to the narrative, he never discusses the glaring problems of the work (e.g., the insertion 8:30-33 and its
relation to its present context), and he makes no attempt to show how the
narrative is structured.

I shall endeavor to discuss four main facets of literary composition, and
thus provide a more comprehensive view of 2 Maccabees as a work
of literature.

1. First, the letters prefixed to the narrative will be examined in order to
   determine their relationship to the epitome.
2. The syntax and style of the narrative will be analysed to uncover the
   literary quality of the work.
3. The structure of the narrative will be sought, and that structure
   examined in light of historical realities. Through this examination of
   structure, certain themes of the author will emerge.
4. The literary character of the work will be determined through comparison with other Hellenistic writings.

After such an analysis, I will discuss questions of date and purpose.

---

[5] J. G. Bunge, *Untersuchungen zum zweiten Makkabäerbuch. Quellen-kritische, literarische, chronologische und historische Untersuchungen zum zweiten Makkabäerbuch als
Quelle syrisch-palästinenischer Geschichte im 2 Jh. v. Chr.* (Bonn: Friedrich-Wilhelms-Universität, 1971).

[6] W. Richnow, "Untersuchungen zu Sprache und Stil des 2 Makkabäerbuches. Ein
Beitrag zur hellenistischen Historiographie" (unpublished PhD dissertation, Göttingen, 1967).

[7]Here, and throughout this study, "author" refers to the author of the epitome 2:19-15:39.
When Jason of Cyrene is referred to, it will be by name.

CHAPTER ONE

THE UNITY OF 2 MACCABEES

The first question to pose in analysing a literary work concerns its unity. Is it composed of parts, or is it whole cloth? Since letters are prefixed to the narrative of 2 Maccabees, one has to ask how these prefixed letters are related to the narrative as well as ask if one can discern sources within the narrative itself. I shall discuss the prefixed letters first, before considering the composition of the narrative itself.

A. The Prefixed Letters (1:1—2:18):

The number and extent of the letters in this opening section have been often debated; opinion has variously discerned one to three letters.[1] In 1857, Grimm observed that, in the Hellenistic period, letters end with dates, and that therefore two letters were prefixed of which the first ended with the dating in 1:10a and the second began at 1:10b.[2] Since an article of Bickermann in 1933, scholars have come to a basic consensus on this point.[3] I shall discuss the two letters in turn.

1:1-10a:

This letter contains a praescriptio, initial greetings (1:1b-6), the body of the letter (1:7-9), and concludes with the date of the letter (1:10a).

The initial greeting comprises greeting formulas as well as an extended prayer of the Judean Jews for their Egyptian brethren. The prayer is composed of general benedictions, all framed in the optative. Comparable to this prayer are the initial greetings reported by Fitzmyer from the corpus of

---

[1] Bunge, *Untersuchungen*, 34, n.7. conveniently catalogues the opinions:
3 letters: Bruston, Willrich, Büchler, Laqueuer, Kahrstedt, Bévenot, Buchers, Rinaldi;
2 letters: Grimm, Knabenhauer, Torrey, Winckler, Herkenne, Kugler, Abel, Penna, Zeitlin;
1 letter: Grätz, Niese, Kolbe.
[2] Grimm, 35-36.
[3] E. Bickermann, "Ein jüdischer Festbrief vom Jahre 124 v. Chr. " *ZNW* 32 (1933) 233-254.

Aramaic epistolography.[4] For example, "May the God of Heaven be much concerned for the wellbeing of our Lord (Bagohi) at all times, and may he show you favor before Darius the King and the princes of the palace a thousand times more than now, and may he grant you a long life, and may you be happy and prosperous at all times."[5] The prayer in 2 Maccabees is also comparable with the prayer of Paul in his opening thanksgiving in the letter to the Philippians: "And it is my prayer that your love may abound more and more, with knowledge and discernment, so that you may approve what is excellent, and may be pure and blameless for the day of Christ, to the glory and praise of God" (Phil 1:9-11). Like these introductory wishes, the prayer of 2 Macc 1:2-6, framed in optatives, is full of general wishes and hopes. There is no hint of admonition or reproach in its phrases,[6] even in such a phrase as 5b: "May he not forsake you in adversity." Such a wish could belong to any set of benedictions.[7]

The body of the letter contains a quotation from a previous letter written in 143/142 B.C.E. (1:7-8), which describes the plunder and deliverance of Jerusalem; then comes an exhortation to celebrate the festival of this deliverance. The exhortation is to celebrate "the days of the *skēnopēgia* of the month of Kislev." Why is the feast called *skēnopēgia*? This word is a technical term for the Feast of Tabernacles in the LXX (Deut 16:16; 31:10; Zech 14:16-19). Why is it used here? D. Sluys suggested that this reflected a Hebrew text like Neh 8:14, and *skēnopēgia* would translate *ḥag*.[8] The Feast of Tabernacles in the seventh month was sometimes designated by *ḥag*, as at 1 Kgs 8:2. To this example of Sluys, Abel added 2 Chr 5:3 and noted that the Feast of Tabernacles was when Solomon dedicated the Temple. This is a tempting suggestion, but one cannot forget that *ḥag* is never translated in the LXX by *skēnopēgia*. It is always translated by *heortē*, even at 1 Kgs 8:2 and 2 Chr 5:3. *Skēnopēgia* translates *sukkâ*. Why was the Feast of Kislev connected with the Feast of Tabernacles? One thing is certain: it is only here and

---

[4] J. A. Fitzmyer, "Some Notes on Aramaic Epistolography," *JBL* 93 (1974) 214-216.

[5] J. A. Fitzmyer, "Some Notes," 214-215, translating no. 30:1-3 in A. E. Cowley, *Aramaic Papyri of the Fifth Century B.C.* (Oxford: Clarendon, 1923).

[6] Bickermann, Abel, Bunge, and Goldstein have adduced a note of admonition in this prayer to support the thesis that the letters were aimed at drawing away followers of the Oniad temple at Leontopolis and bringing them back to recognition of the Jerusalem temple. But admonitions, as at 2 Chr 30:6-9 and 1 Chr 28:7-10 (Bunge, *Untersuchungen*, 596, even suggests that 2 Macc 1:2-6 paraphrases 1 Chr 28:7-10) contain imperatives and threats, not optatives.

[7] Cf. LXX Sir 51:10-12; LXX Ps 36:33; 139:9. Tcherikover also holds that there is no specific referent in this wish: V. Tcherikover and A. Fuks, *Corpus Papyrorum Judaicorum* (Cambridge: Harvard Univ., 1957) 1.23-24, fn.58.

[8] D. Sluys, *De Maccabaeorum Libris I et II Quaestiones* (Amsterdam: J. Clausen, 1904) 66.

at 2 Macc 1:18 and 10:6 that such a connection is made.[9]

What is striking about this festal letter is its lopsidedness. The long opening prayer takes up half the document, and makes the whole letter top-heavy. Furthermore, the references to Jason and to the Feast of Tabernacles in Kislev, no doubt intelligible to the receivers of the letters, would today have no meaning without the narrative of the epitome. One suspects that the letter has been edited, and passages relevant to the narrative of 2 Maccabees selected. This would also help explain the presence of the verb *katallassein* in the prayer at 2 Macc 1:5b. Without the epitome, this use of *katallassein*, particularly in a prayer replete with traditional Jewish blessings, would be unique in Hellenistic Jewish usage till the time of Paul and Josephus. In the LXX, *katallassein* is found in most manuscripts at LXX Jer 31:39, but, following the parallelism, the meaning is "turn around," rather than "reconcile." Apart from this passage in Jeremiah, the verb is found in the LXX only at 2 Macc 7:33 and 8:29. The noun *katallagē* is found at 2 Macc 5:20. The verb is used programmatically in 2 Maccabees—in a reflection over the behavior of Antiochus IV (5:17-20), in the prophetic speech of the youngest martyr (7:33), and after the first major victory of the Jews accomplished through the help of God (8:29).

Although there is no express cross-reference of any kind between this first letter and the epitome, there is thus clear evidence of some connection between the two. Not only is there the linguistic connection of *katallassein*, but there is also the thematic congruence. The body of the letter describes the plunder and deliverance of Jerusalem, and exhorts the Egyptian Jewry to celebrate this festival. As we shall see, this topos of attack and relief runs throughout the epitome. I therefore suggest that an authentic festal letter has been edited and prefixed to the epitome.

---

[9] At 2 Macc 10:6, the technical term is not used and applied to the festival of purification, but it is simply stated: "They celebrated it with gladness for eight days in the manner of (dwellers in) tents, remembering how, a little while before, at the feast of Tabernacles, they had been wandering in the mountains and caverns like wild animals." This last phrase is a clear reference back to 2 Macc 5:27 which described how Judas and his companions lived after the flight from persecution. 2 Macc 10:6 has several nuances: usually the phrase *skēnōmatōn tropon* is translated "like the feast of Tabernacles" (Grimm, Abel, Habicht). However, *skēnōma* is never used to designate the feast of Tabernacles in the LXX or Philo: the term used is *skēnē* or *skēnopēgia* or the phrase *hē tōn skēnōn heortē*, as in the same verse 2 Macc 10:6. On the other hand, if what was meant was simply that the feasters lived in tents, *skēnōmatōn tropon* is a clumsy way of expressing this. The use of *tropon* + genitive must be connected with the phrase of the same verse, *thēriōn tropon*. The dwelling in tents is thus to remember their nomad-like existence in the mountains during the occupation, as the feast of Tabernacles itself was to remind the people "that I made the people of Israel dwell in tents when I brought them out of the land of Egypt" (Lev 23:43). As the feast of Tabernacles celebrated the redemption from

1:10b-2:18:

While the letter of 1:10a is cryptic in its brevity, the letter which begins at 1:10b causes problems because of its length. The first major difficulty arises from the account of the death of Antiochus IV in 1:13-16.[10] It clearly deviates from the account of the death in 2 Maccabees 9, where the attempted sacrilege takes place at Persepolis. The account in 1:13-16 also diverges from the manner of Antiochus IV's death as told in Polybius 31.9, Appian *Syriaca* 66, 1 Macc 6:1-16, and 2 Maccabees 9. All these sources agree that Antiochus IV did not die at the assault on the temple. but some time later. In Appian, he dies of consumption; in Polybius, of madness which some say was brought on by divine displeasure; in 1 and 2 Maccabees by disease brought on by the Jewish God. While 1:13-16 agrees with the other sources against 2 Maccabees 9 in that it places the assault at Elymais,[11] it contains a divergent, and quite bloody, account of the death itself of Antiochus IV. A similar divergency occurs between Appian's account, where Antiochus is successful in plundering the temple, and the others, where he fails.[12] One should not be alarmed at such divergency. It is present in the accounts of the death of Antiochus III: according to Diodorus Siculus 29.15 (cf. 28.3), Antiochus III was successful in his plunder of the temple of Bel at Elymais, but was punished later by the gods; in Justin 32.1.2, he dies with his whole army at the attempt on the temple. Such divergent accounts of the deaths of great men are not unusual—note, for example, the various accounts of the death of Alexander the Great and Themistocles.[13] What is surprising, however, is to find the two accounts in 2 Maccabees without any relation made between them. Would the author of the epitome, had he known of the account at 1:13-16, have completely

Egypt, so the feast in 2 Macc 10:6 celebrated the redemption from the oppression of Antiochus IV.

[10] Attempts to show that 2 Macc 1:13-17 narrate the death of Antiochus III or of Antiochus VII Sidetes are unsuccessful. The argument of C. C. Torrey for Antiochus VII Sidetes ("Die Briefe 2 Makk. 1,1-2,18" *ZAW* 20 [1900] 225-242; "The Letters Prefixed to Second Maccabees," *JAOS* 60 [1940] 119-150) presupposes, among other things, that the letter was written in 124 B.C.E. Against Antiochus III, see M. Holleaux, *Études d'épigraphie et d'histoire grecques* (Paris: E. de Boccard, 1942) 3.255-279.

[11] W. W. Tarn (*The Greeks in Bactria and India* [Cambridge: Cambridge Univ., 1951] 29.463-466) suggested that Artemis is the Elamite goddess Nanaea, and that her temple was at Susa. O. Mørkholm (*Antiochus IV of Syria* [Copenhagen: Gylendal, 1966] 170, fn.15) noted that Strabo (15.3.2-4; 16.1.18) distinguished Susa from Elymais. However, as Walbank (*A Historical Commentary on Polybius* [Oxford: Clarendon, 1979] 3.473) states, "the two are often confused in Hellenistic times, and Tarn may be right." See Weissbach, "Elymais" *PW* 5.2458-67; Gray, "Elymais" *OCD²* 381.

[12] Finally, in Appian it is the temple of Aphrodite, in Polybius that of Artemis.

[13] Plu *Life of Alexander* 76-77; Cicero *Brutus* 43.

ignored it in his version? Bunge, following Schunck, tries to show that the author of the epitome did not ignore it, but that the letter caused a fundamental restructuring of the epitome. The author of the epitome, on reading the letter, would have thought that the death of Antiochus IV came before the purification of the temple.[14] This would have moved him to place the death of Antiochus IV before the purification of the temple, i.e., to have inserted 2 Maccabees 9 before 2 Macc 10:1-8.[15] This theory will be discussed below and found wanting;[16] the letter did not cause a radical displacement in the text of the epitome. Even so, it would still not answer the objection that the accounts are quite divergent. Such a theory also assumes that the letter of 1:10b was written prior to the purification, an assumption recently challenged by A. Momigliano and more fully by B. Z. Wacholder.[17]

Whether 1:18b-2:15 is an interpolation to an original letter or not,[18] one still has to investigate how it relates to the epitome. That this section is composed of many elements is clearly seen. First comes a long discussion on the fire at the time of Nehemiah (1:18-36), then a section on Jeremiah (2:1-8), a comparison between Moses and Solomon (2:9-12), a reference to the founding of a library by Nehemiah and Judas' imitation of this (2:13-15), and finally the conclusion (2:16-18).

The first section (1:18-36) is concerned to show the continuity between the temple of Nehemiah and that of Solomon. The fire from the first temple had, over the years, turned to a heavy liquid. Nehemiah ordered that this liquid be poured over the wood and the sacrifices; when the sun shone on it, fire burst out and the sacrifices were consumed. By means of this astounding

---

[14] Bunge, *Untersuchungen*, 278-287.

[15] Bunge (*Untersuchungen*, 492-501) recognizes that Antiochus IV died before the feast of 25th Kislev, as BM 35603 has shown, but he holds that this feast was not when the temple was purified. According to Bunge, the temple was purified after the victory over Nicanor/Gorgias and, at that time, a festival to commemorate the uncelebrated festival of Tabernacles was held. Such a festival would have later been replaced by the festival of 25th Kislev, held in lieu of the abominable celebration of Antiochus IV's birthday. The basis for positing such a feast is Bunge's own historical reconstruction of events, and falls with it. A Momigliano ("The Second Book of Maccabees," *Classical Philology* 70 [1975] 82) holds that such a theory cannot be proved.

[16] See chapter 3.

[17] A. Momigliano, "The Second Book," 81; B. Z. Wacholder, "The Letter from Judah Maccabee to Aristobulus: Is 2 Maccabees 1:10b-2:18 Authentic?" *HUCA* 49 (1978) 100.

[18] That it is an interpolation: D. Sluys, *De Maccabaeorum libris*, 68; W. Brownlee, "Maccabees, Books of," *IDB* 3.208; Bunge, *Untersuchungen*, 58-62; 99-104. Against an interpolation: B. Z. Wacholder, "The Letter," 112-117. Wacholder's suggestion that "the fire" of 1:18b, a reference which has always been difficult, refers to a feast of fire, a semi-feast of eight days during the Second Temple period which commemorated the establishment of the daily burnt offerings, is very tempting.

event, sacrifice could be resumed in Jerusalem.[19] While the story propounds this continuity, it also tells of the discovery of naphtha, that fiery liquid known to Hellenistic scientists and geographers as pertaining to Babylonia.[20] It was particularly well known through the story of Alexander the Great and the boy Stephanus, who smeared himself with the naphtha, caught fire, and barely escaped with his life.[21] That 2 Macc 1:18-36 deals with naphtha is clear not only from the name (1:36: *nephthar, nephthai*),[22] but also from the way it works. At 1:22, fire breaks out when the sun shines on it. The same happens when the remaining liquid is poured over the rocks: as soon as the light from the altar shines on it, it burst into flame. The nature of naphtha is to draw fire to itself. Dioscorides says: "It can so catch fire that it can draw fire from a distance." Plutarch comments "This naphtha . . . is so liable to catch fire, that before it touches the flame it will kindle at the very light that surrounds it, and often inflame the intermediate air also."[23] 2 Macc 1:32 should be translated: "When this was done, a flame was kindled; when the light from the altar shone forth, (the naphtha) was consumed."[24]

Once it is recognized that the continuity of the second temple with the first is through the discovery of naphtha, this story must be classed with other efforts by Jews to show that their heroes were the first inventors and discoverers of things useful to mankind, the *prōtoi euretai*. Artapanus claimed that Moses had invented ships, earth-moving equipment and military weapons, and also that he had a hand in the founding of Egyptian

---

[19] Torrey attempts to locate the whole story in Babylonia. One of his major arguments is based on the presence of *tote* in 1:18, the reading of A′ 62-542. However, this is not the reading of most manuscripts, and Hanhart's critical edition does not include it. Torrey's whole discussion is dominated by the desire to show that the author of the piece could not have been so stupid as to have Nehemiah, rather than Ezra, building the altar at Jerusalem. While I admit the strangeness of the attribution to Nehemiah, to locate a temple in Babylonia without any other evidence is even more rash.

[20] Dioscorides, *De materia medica* 1.73 (1st cent. c.e.). Strabo 15.3.15. Eratosthenes, as quoted by Strabo 16.1.15. Plu *Life of Alexander* 35. Pliny *HN* 2.109.235.

[21] Plu *Life of Alexander* 35.

[22] The plausible etymology derives the word from the Persian *naft*, while "naphtar" would represent an adaptation to the Hebrew *tŏhŏrâ*. Cf. Lev 14:1, where this word is connected with purifying waters. See F. M. Abel and J. Starcky, *Les Livres des Maccabées* (La Sainte Bible; 3rd ed.; Paris: Cerf, 1961) note to 2 Macc 1:36.

[23] Dioscorides, *De materia medica* (ed. M. Wellmann; Berlin: Weidmann, 1958) 1.73. Plu *Life of Alexander* 35.

[24] Part of the trouble in translating this verse has been caused by the omission of the subject of *edapanēthē*, and commentators have taken the subject to be *phlox*. This does not produce any meaningful translation. Rather than looking for a second miracle, one is justified, on the parallel of 2 Macc 1:22 and the nature of naphtha, to allow that the author omitted the subject or rather, referred to a subject which is not the nearest, i.e., the naphtha.

religion.[25] Abraham too was the inventor or discoverer of astrology and the Chaldean science.[26] In the story of 2 Maccabees, Nehemiah and his companions are the discoverers of naphtha—they give it its name. The interpretation of naphtha as purification is secondary, and serves to link the discovery with the feast of Kislev. This festival in Kislev is thus a fire festival, a description present in Josephus,[27] but completely absent from the narratives of 1 and 2 Maccabees.[28]

To this fiery story, other elements have been added in an associative fashion.[29] Chap. 2:1 gives another version of the preceding story and specifies that it was Jeremiah himself who told the priests to take the fire. Jeremiah could not be mentioned without reference to prophetic exhortation to follow the Law and avoid idols.[30] The mention of Jeremiah attracts another story about the prophet at the time of exile, but one which has nothing to do with the festival of fire, a story in fact which in part contradicts the earlier story. While the previous story had been concerned to show the continuity between the first and the second temple, this story of Jeremiah emphasizes the discontinuity between the two. The ark, the tent, and the altar of incense are hidden and will not be found until God works the ingathering of his people (2:7-8). At that time, the glory and the cloud will appear. This is quite a separate tradition from that of the fire burning on the altar. In the final words of Jeremiah, reference is made to Moses and Solomon (2:8). Verses 9-12 pick up this reference, and develop the similarities between the two leaders. The final similarity noted, that of celebrating a feast for eight days, leads back to the activity of Nehemiah. Alongside Nehemiah's activity in collecting the writings of Judaism is placed the similar activity of Judas.

All these traditions are placed side by side in what may appear to be superficial links, but in reality they refract and heighten the rich, colorful tapestry of tradition associated with the installation of the temple. The past theophanic events at the time of Moses and Solomon fuse with future hopes of restoration, hopes which were somewhat realized at the time of Nehe-

---

[25] Artapanus, FGH 726 F3 (Eusebius, *Praep.Ev.* 9.27.4-6).

[26] (Ps.-)Eupolemus FGH 724 Fl (Eusebius, *Praep.Ev.* 9.17.3).

[27] Jos *Ant* 12.325.

[28] Attempts to give such a miraculous turn to the phrase at 2 Macc 10:3, *purōsantes lithous*, are groundless.

[29] Somewhat analogous to the fashion of midrash. See A. G. Wright, *The Literary Genre Midrash* (New York: St. Paul, 1967) 65-66, although Wright has a rather narrow definition of midrash and holds that it must be a comment on a biblical text.

[30] The *Epistula Ieremiae* strongly warns against the idols of Babylonia: 2 Macc 2:1-3 would seem to be what prophets are supposed to do rather than a specific reference to the *Epistula Ieremiae*. See W. Naumann, "Untersuchungen über den apokryphen Jeremiasbrief," BZAW 25 (1913) 52-53; Bunge, *Untersuchungen* 116-117.

miah. These rich traditions give depth and meaning to the feast of the Purification. Such a cluster of traditions cannot be regarded as a "reasoned attack upon challenges to the holiness of the second temple prevalent at the time."[31] The tradition of first fire is no doubt propaganda, but such an etiological story does not answer any objections against the pollution of the temple committed under Antiochus IV.

This feast is conceived as a festival of fire. The idea that Nehemiah and his followers were the discoverers of naphtha, that naphtha is the medium through which the sacred fire on the altar is rekindled, all these emphasize the importance of fire. Such an emphasis may be derived from Persian influence, for Strabo clearly links naphtha with Persian religion.[32] What is clear is that such traditions find no echo in 1 Maccabees and the epitome of 2 Maccabees.

Nor is there an echo of the theme of eschatological expectation which runs through this second letter. In the prayer of Nehemiah, God is asked to "gather together our scattered people," to plant his people in his holy place (2 Macc 1:27-29). Jeremiah declares that the tent and the ark and the altar of incense will be hidden and their place unknown "until God gathers his people together again and shows his mercy" (2 Macc 2:7). The letter ends with the hope "that God will soon have mercy upon us and will gather us from everywhere under heaven into his holy place" (2 Macc 2:18).[33]

The language of the second letter also evidences differences from the epitome. The second letter is full of Semiticisms: the phrases *paratassō en* (= *nlḥm b* at LXX Judg B 8:1; 9:45; 11:9.12.27; 12:1.3; Zech 14:13; 1 Esdr 15:8 [= Neh 4:2]); *melē poiēsantes* (1:16), the use of *edōke* at 1:17, the absence of *epi* before *lithous* at 1:31,[34] the use of *kai* to introduce the apodosis at 1:33 and 2:6, and the pleonasm, *elambane kai metedidou*, at 1:35. These Semiticisms throughout 2 Macc 1:10b-2:18 contrast with the narrative of the epitome where there is little evidence for Semiticisms.[35] When these linguistic features are combined with the fact that the content of the letter is so different from the epitome both in its account of the death of Antiochus IV and in its treatment of the Feast of Purification as a festival of

---

[31] J. A. Goldstein, *1 Maccabees* (AB 41; Garden City, NY: Doubleday, 1976) 546.

[32] Strabo 15.3.15: "They also have Pyraetheia, enclosures worthy of note. In the midst of these is an altar on which there is a large amount of ashes and where the Magi maintain an ever-burning fire." These temples are found in Cappadocia, and near the summer residence of the Persian king.

[33] For the eschatological note associated with *episynagō*, see W. Schrage *TDNT* 7.842.

[34] P. Katz ("The Text of 2 Maccabees Reconsidered," *ZNW* 51 [1960] 13) restores *epi*, stating that the corruption is due to haplography: *ekeleus(E)EPIlithous*. As Katz himself concedes, however, the absence of *epi* in a translated Greek text would be a Hebraism.

[35] See chapter 2 for a discussion of Semiticisms in the epitome.

fire with a rich cluster of traditions, one is led to the conclusion that the letter is not from the author of the epitome. However, the very richness of the traditions about the sanctity of the Temple and even the insistence in the account of the death of Antiochus IV that it was by divine retribution—such only serve to forge links with the epitome. Though not by the same author, they are certainly compatible. And such a compatibility must have led to their having been combined.

Polemic Against the Temple at Leontopolis:

One final note about the introductory letters. I see no evidence of polemic against the temple at Leontopolis. The attempts of Bunge and others to find a purpose for the writing of 2 Maccabees in such a polemic presupposes a debate that does not exist. Bunge, in particular, tries to find evidence for such pro- and anti-Leontopolis feeling in the LXX use of the term *Ōn*.[36] Leontopolis would equal *Oniou chōra* (Strabo uses this term in Jos *Ant* 12.287) and this would respond to *Ōn*. Such connections, however, are simply not there. T. O. Lambdin has shown that *Ōn* is an acceptable Hebraicization of the Egyptian name of the city. "The Egyptian called the city *iwnw* (or *ʾinw*), which is borrowed in Hebrew as *ʾÔn* (also *Aven*) and in cuneiform inscriptions as *Anu* (Middle Babylonian) and *Unu* (Late Assyrian)."[37] At Exod 1:11, Heliopolis = *Ōn* and this identification explains the presence of *Ōn* at Jer LXX 50:13 (MT 43:13). As for the other places where *Ōn* occurs in the LXX (Hos 4:15; 5:8; 10:5.8; 12:4; Amos 1:5), these occurrences can be explained by the desire of the translator to keep a proper noun, rather than attempt to maintain the pun where *ʾwn* equals wealth or wickedness or Bethel.[38] Polemic against Leontopolis is not present.[39]

As opposed to such speculation, the thesis of J. Collins argues that Book 3 of the Sibylline Oracles, clear pro-Jerusalem Temple propaganda of the 2nd cent. B.C.E., stems from the Jewish community at Leontopolis.[40]

---

[36] Bunge, *Untersuchungen*, 583-594.

[37] T. O. Lambdin, "Heliopolis," *IDB* 2.579.

[38] Cf. R. B. Coote, "Hosea XII," *VT* 21 (1971) 393-394.

[39] Bunge also makes use of Isa 19:18, where the LXX has *polis asedek* while the MT reads *ʿyr hḥrs*, as pro-Leontopolis propaganda. However, the very fact that the LXX leaves the Hebrew untranslated would seem to argue, if anything, that there is no polemic against Leontopolis. One suspects, in fact, that the LXX author wished to leave the location undetermined.

[40] J. J. Collins, *The Sibylline Oracles of Egyptian Judaism* (SBLDS 13; Missoula: Scholars Press, 1974) 48-55.

Such a thesis clearly undermines any attempt to portray relations between Leontopolis and Jerusalem as hostile.[41]

Conclusion:

What has been shown so far is that the first letter shows signs of editing to align it with the epitome: the use of *katallassō*, the cryptic brevity of the body of the letter, the meaninglessness of the references to events without the narrative of the epitome. All these point to purposeful connections being made between the first letter and the epitome. The second letter diverges strongly from the epitome, but reflects the emphasis, basic to the epitome, that the temple is holy and that God defends it and takes vengeance on its attackers. While the epitome, therefore, must be considered an independent work and studied as such, one will also have to agree that the final arrangement of the work with the two letters prefixed is no coincidence.

B. Source Analysis of the Epitome

Within the narrative of the epitome itself, scholars have attempted to discern sources. If one could uncover the remnants of various sources in 2 Maccabees, this would say a great deal about the literary character of the work. One is therefore compelled to deal with this question. Of course, one already knows that there are sources in 2 Maccabees: the letters in 2 Maccabees 9 and 11 are used as sources.[42] 2 Maccabees is an epitome of a larger historical work: Jason of Cyrene is a source for the narrative content. The source criticism of 2 Maccabees has lately focused on the question of whether there is another source discernible behind the work of Jason of Cyrene—a biography of Judas Maccabeus. It is to this discussion that I will first turn. After evaluating this, I will discuss suggestions that there are doublets in 2 Maccabees 3 and 6, and that 2 Maccabees 7 was added later to the narrative framework.

---

[41] I do not see any polemic in the titles applied to Aristobulus at 2 Macc 1:10b, "the teacher of King Ptolemy, and who is of the race of the anointed priests." Commentators have seen in this last phrase polemic against the Oniad temple, for the letter is being addressed to a member of the Zadokite/Oniad line, who is not Onias IV. If this is anti-Oniad propaganda, it is extremely subtle. One reason why such a fulsome phrase might have been applied to Aristobulus is sheer flattery.

[42] These could, of course, have been present in the work of Jason of Cyrene.

B. 1. The Biography of Judas:

Since both 1 and 2 Maccabees treat of the actions of Judas Maccabeus, it is not surprising that their accounts overlap. Some scholars, however, have inferred from this overlap that a written source, a biography of Judas, lies behind the two accounts. The most exhaustive work done on this problem has been that of K. D. Schunck and that of J. G. Bunge.[43] Bunge professes to build on the work of Schunck, albeit with modifications.[44] I shall therefore deal with Bunge's work, but the same observations will apply, *mutatis mutandis*, to the results of Schunck.

Both Schunck and Bunge strongly emphasize that one cannot separate sources in 2 Maccabees or even in 1 Maccabees on linguistic grounds.[45] The inability to find linguistic correspondence between 1 and 2 Maccabees, even though they are supposed to be using a common source, is explained by Bunge as due to the history of transmission: on the one hand, the originally Hebrew life of Judas would have been used by the author of 1 Maccabees, and then 1 Maccabees would have been translated into Greek;[46] on the other side, Jason of Cyrene would have used the life of Judas in his Greek history, which was then shortened. A favorite phrase of Bunge's is: "substantiell aus der Judasvita stammen." One should not expect, according to Bunge, to find words in common between 1 and 2 Maccabees. Already one begins to sense that source criticism is being applied here in an unusual way.

The approach of Bunge is to compare the parallel events in 1 and 2 Maccabees. Coincidences in the telling of one or more events is not important, but rather the ordering of such coincidences is what is looked for. If a series of events is related in exactly the same order, this argues for a common source.[47] When Bunge talks of a common source for 1 and 2 Maccabees, he is not talking of a linguistic influence on the way the stories are told, but of a common order of events. At the beginning of his investigation, Bunge claimed that there was a correspondence in detail beyond what could be expected from two works treating the same historical events, and that such a correspondence forced one to posit a common source for the two works.[48]

---

[43] K. D. Schunck, *Die Quellen des I. und II. Makkabäerbuches* (Halle: Niemeyer, 1954). Bunge, *Untersuchungen*, 206-329.

[44] Bunge, *Untersuchungen*, 293-298.

[45] Bunge, *Untersuchungen*, 213: "Eine wörtliche Quellenscheidung hält er (Schunck) infolge der redaktionellen Arbeit des Verfassers I. Makk. natürlich auch für unmöglich. Dem ist voll zuzustimmen." 215: "Das Griechisch des 2 Makk ist in allen Teilen des Buches sehr einheitlich, und es ist uns nicht möglich, hier irgendwelche terminologische Unterschiede aufzuspüren."

[46] Bunge, *Untersuchungen*, 214.

[47] Bunge, *Untersuchungen*, 217.

[48] Bunge, *Untersuchungen*, 207-208.

However, his argument simply does not stand up to examination.

To show this failure on every point would be tedious and would divert us from the main purpose of our work. An example comparison between the narratives in 1 Maccabees 5 and 2 Maccabees 12 is interesting. Schematically, there appears to be a basic similarity in the arrangement of the towns named:

2 Maccabees (from 12:10)	*1 Maccabees* (from 5:24)
the Arabs	Nabateans
Kaspin	Bosora
Toubiani	Toubiani
unknown fortress	Kaspho, Maked, Bosor
Karnaim	Karnaim
Ephron	Ephron
Scythopolis	(mention of Beth-shan)
Jerusalem	Jerusalem
Idumea/Marisa	Idumea: Hebron, Marisa
Adullam	Azotus

In the earlier sections of these chapters, to the detailed description of the outrages of Joppa and the plans of Jamnia against their Jewish citizens in 2 Macc 12:3-9 corresponds the general statement in 1 Macc 5:2 that the heathen round about resolved to destroy the Jews and began to kill and ravage them. Similar, though not identical, incidents to those narrated at 1 Macc 5:3-8 are found at 2 Macc 10:15-38. 1 Macc 5:9-23 deals mainly with preliminaries to the events at 1 Macc 5:24-68. Within the narrative of these events, 2 Maccabees places Kaspin before the meeting with the Toubiani, 1 Maccabees places Kaspho after the meeting. Such a corresponding list of events in its stark nakedness is impressive, but one has to state that this list is all that is in common. The narration of events at each incident is entirely different. For example, in three episodes (1 Macc 5:55-62; 65-68; 2 Macc 12:32-45) it is reported that there were Jewish casualties.[49] Marisa is mentioned both in 1 Macc 5:66 and 2 Macc 12:35, but, in 1 Maccabees, it is a town that Judas passes by. In 2 Maccabees, it is the town to which Gorgias flees, whereas in 1 Macc 5:59, Gorgias is well in control of Jamnia, quite far from Marisa. 1 Macc 5:65-68 and 2 Macc 12:32-45 are campaigns to the south, while 1 Macc 5:55-62 is a campaign to the north. But while in 1 Macc 5:65-68 Judas attacks Hebron, then passes through Marisa and on to Azotus, the action of 2 Macc 12:32-45 is outside Marisa and Judas visits Adullam. The campaigns are related in very different ways. All that is in common is the

---

[49] The name of the junior officer may also be the same: 1 Macc 5:60 *Azarias*; 2 Macc 12:36 *Esdrin*. The functions in the story are quite different, however.

name Gorgias and the town Marisa. Gorgias in 2 Maccabees is the governor of Idumea, while in 1 Maccabees he commands the forces of Jamnia, and Marisa plays a very different role in the two accounts. The corresponding list of names and places that one finds behind 1 Macc 5:24-68 and 2 Macc 12:10-45 is no more than one would expect to find in similar treatments of the same historical events and does not force one to posit a written source behind the two accounts.

Another example might be the narrative of the expedition of Nicanor and Gorgias in 2 Macc 8:9-36 and 1 Macc 3:38-4:25. Here too close examination shows no need to posit a life of Judas behind the accounts. Both have the same personages, although 1 Maccabees emphasizes the role of Gorgias, 2 Maccabees that of Nicanor. Both accounts mention the presence of slave-traffickers among the Seleucid army (1 Macc 3:41; 2 Macc 8:10-11.25), a common practice in the Hellenistic world. 1 Maccabees details the tactical maneuvers: Judas and his forces escape from a surprise attack of a detachment of Gorgias (4:1-2), they attack and scatter the enemy's camp (4:12-15), and then the first group of enemy forces flees when they see their camp plundered and pillaged (4:19-22). In 2 Maccabees there are no such maneuvers—one pitched battle decides all. The prayers before the battles (1 Macc 3:58-60; 4:8-11; 2 Macc 8:16-20) are full of commonplaces—the exhortation not to fear, the call on God to remember his past covenant. 1 Macc 4:9 exemplifies God's past help by recalling the destruction of Pharaoh and his army at the Red Sea, while 2 Macc 8:20 recalls the havoc wreaked on the army of Sennacherib and the aid given at some unknown battle with the Galatians when the Jews fought alongside some Macedonians.[50] These different examples lead one to suspect that there is no common written source behind the two accounts.

The most conclusive factor, however, lies in the different order of events. In 1 Maccabees, Judas and the community assemble at Mizpah, they pray and open the Torah scrolls; the army is then divided, with commanders of thousands, hundreds, fifties, and tens, with the rules of Deut 20:1-9 for non-combatants being observed. The army then marches off to Emmaus, Judas exhorts his forces, and then the tactical maneuvers begin. In 2 Maccabees, on the other hand, the cowardly leave when news first arrives (8:13), Judas exhorts his army, the army is divided into four, the Scriptures are read, and then battle is joined. The whole episode at Mizpah is missing from

---

[50] The precise identification of this battle is still uncertain, but the conjecture of I. Levy that *Bagadonia* be read instead of *Babylōnia* at 2 Macc 8:20, and thus the reference be to the victory of Antiochus I in 275 B.C.E. against the Gauls, is brilliant. I. Levy, "Notes d'histoire hellénistique sur le second Livre des Maccabées," *Annuaire de l'Institut de Philologie et d'Histoire Orientales et Slaves. Bruxelles* 10 (1950) 681-699.

2 Maccabees. The order as well as the content differs. All that is in common between the two accounts, once one excises the commonplace topoi of prayer and exhortation, is that Nicanor/Gorgias came and were defeated.

In conclusion, then, Bunge's insistence that the order of events in 1 and 2 Maccabees forces one to posit a common written source to explain this similarity in fact leads to the opposite of what he wants. For often the order of events is not the same, and, when it is, the only point in common is the list of names. Such does not make for a source for the accounts as we have them, and can more easily be explained by holding that the events are related in basically the same order because of the general agreement that that is how they occurred.

As a tool for further source criticism, Bunge proposes to distinguish between the two phrases used to refer to the hero in 2 Maccabees: *Ioudas* and *ho Makkabaios*. From a list of their occurrences, Bunge concludes that two sources are at hand, since *Ioudas* is mentioned mainly in 2 Maccabees 12 through 15, while *ho Makkabaios* is used throughout 2 Maccabees 10 and 11. On closer investigation, he concludes that *ho Makkabaios* betrays the author of 2 Maccabees, while *Ioudas* reflects the author of the life of Judas.[51] The use of different epithets to describe a character can be a valuable tool, but it has to be supported by other criteria as, e.g., the presence of doublets, or stylistic changes.[52] In 2 Maccabees, however, these epithets occur within stylistically indistinguishable passages. For example, within a *men/de* construction at 2 Macc 15:6-7, one finds *Ioudas* in the *men* clause, *ho Makkabaios* in the *de*. One cannot distinguish verse from verse here. Again, the epithet *Ioudas* is found at 2 Macc 12:36-45, a passage which clearly betrays re-writing by the author of the epitome.[53] Should not one have expected *ho*

---

[51] Bunge, *Untersuchungen*, 263; 271-272. Bunge lists the usages:
Ioudas: 8:12; 12:5.11bis.12.14.15.21.22.23.36.38.39.42; 13:1.10.12.20.23; 14:1.10.11.14.17.18.22. 24.26.33; 15:1.6.15.17.26.
ho Makkabaios: 8:5.16; 10:16.19.21.25.30.33.35; 11:6.7.15; 12:19.20; 13:24; 14:27.30; 15:7.21.
Ioudas ho Makkabaios: 2:19; 14:6.
Ioudas ho kai Makkabaios: 5:27; 8:1.
Makkabaios: 10:1.

[52] Suggestions of D. Arenhoevel and M. Zambelli are based on even slimmer evidence. Arenhoevel (*Die Theokratie nach dem 1. und 2. Makkabäerbuch* [Mainz: Matthias-Grunewald, 1967] 108) suggests that the use of *Makkabaios*, not *ho Makkabaios*, at 2 Macc 10:1 reveals the hand of a redactor later than the author of the epitome. Zambelli ("La composizione del secondo libro dei Maccabei e la nuova cronologia di Antioco IV Epifane," *Miscellanea Greca e Romana* [Studi pubblicati dall'Istituto Italiano per la Storia Antica 16; Rome, 1965] 284-287) posits that 2 Maccabees divides into two distinct parts: 2 Maccabees 3-11, which derives from Jason of Cyrene, and 2 Maccabees 12-15, which comes from another source. The basis for this thesis is that absolute dates occur at 2 Macc 13:1 and 14:4, but relative dates occur elsewhere. Such suggestions take no account of stylistic factors.

[53] So Bunge also, *Untersuchungen*, 249-252.

Makkabaios in this of all places? The same could be said of other places. Bunge has been right to notice this change of epithets, but his explanation of why they occur as they do is not convincing. The consistent use of *Ioudas* in 2 Maccabees 12-13 and of *ho Makkabaios* in 2 Maccabees 10-11 should alert one to the possibility, not of separate sources, but of major editorial re-working.

The Death of Persecutors:

J. A. Goldstein has recently mounted a search for sources in 2 Maccabees. He posits two major sources, one a history of the Oniads by Onias IV, the other a work similar in genre to Lactantius' *On the Death of Persecutors* and labelled by Goldstein DMP.[54]

Goldstein was led to posit the Oniad history when he tried to find a source for the chapters in 2 Maccabees which have no parallel in 1 Maccabees and which deal with the Oniads, Onias III and Jason, and their usurper, Menelaus. Goldstein detects in these chapters a pro-Oniad bias coupled with a disbelief in the inviolability of the Jerusalem temple, two traits which Goldstein holds best fit Onias IV. Onias IV would be concerned to uphold the honor of his family, and as founder of the Leontopolis temple, would be against Jerusalem. Such biases are not present in 2 Maccabees 3 and 4. This is clear even in Goldstein's main "proof"-text, 2 Macc 3:1: "When the holy city was inhabited in perfect peace and the laws were strictly observed because of the piety of Onias, the high-priest, and his hatred of wickedness." Goldstein holds that this passage shows that the temple is not inviolable; the temple is at peace only because of the holiness of Onias. This further means, according to Goldstein, that the temple is not the connecting point between man and God, but the Oniad priesthood is. It would thus be pro-Leontopolis propaganda.[55] This view is simply not there. Throughout 2 Maccabees, the author is at pains to show that the temple is protected only as long as the Jews follow the laws of God. This is stated explicitly at 2 Macc 8:36, which Goldstein attributes to Jason of Cyrene, and most of all in the aphorism of 5:19: "The Lord did not select the nation for the sake of the place, but the place for the sake of the nation." This verse, as all of 5:15-20, Goldstein attributed to his other source, DMP, because it maintains the inviolability of the temple.[56] Such reasoning is in clear violation of the text. Goldstein finds

---

[54] J. A. Goldstein, *1 Maccabees*, 92. "The Tales of the Tobiads," *Christianity, Judaism, and other Greco-Roman Cults. III* (ed. J. Neusner; Festschrift M. Smith; Leiden: Brill, 1975) 85-123.

[55] Goldstein, *1 Maccabees*, 57-58.

[56] Goldstein, *1 Maccabees*, 102, fn. 47.

other pro-Oniad propaganda at 2 Macc 4:5: "Onias . . . resorted to the king, not to be an accuser of his fellow-citizens, but as looking after the welfare, public and private, of all the people." Goldstein sees this as an apologia for Onias III's trip to the king. Is this necessary, however? Onias' attitude contrasts strongly with the behavior of Simon and his associates, who have acted as informants against the people (2 Macc 4:1) and who have resorted to murder (2 Macc 4:3). Also, the author of the epitome loves to use antithesis: cf. 2 Macc 5:6: "Jason, . . . *not regarding* that success gained over one's kindred is the greatest failure, *but* fancying that he was winning trophies from his enemies, not his countrymen." Literarily, there is no need to regard 2 Macc 4:5 as hiding an apologia for the Oniads. The final piece of pro-Oniad propaganda seen by Goldstein is the reference to Hyrcanus, son of Tobias (2 Macc 3:11). But would only an Oniad partisan have mentioned this fact?[57] The reference to Hyrcanus would, according to Goldstein, remind readers of the successful pro-Ptolemaic policy of the Tobiads, and be another attack against the Seleucids. The text, which stresses the kindly reception of Heliodorus by Onias and mentions Hyrcanus only to underline the respectability of what is going on in the Temple treasury, simply does not support Goldstein's theory. As shown above, the temple at Leontopolis was not violently opposed to that at Jerusalem, and so the other leg of Goldstein's theory also falls.

As for the DMP, this too is not based on real evidence from the text. The starting point for Goldstein is the chronological difficulty posed by 2 Macc 13:1 and 14:1.4. The events of 2 Maccabees 13 take place in the "hundred and forty-ninth year," those of 2 Macc 14:1-2 *meta trietē chronon*, and those of 2 Macc 14:4 "in the hundred and fifty-first year." Goldstein rejects the solution of most scholars that one interpret *trietē* as referring to the year series 151-150-149, and suggests that 2 Maccabees 14 links with 2 Maccabees 12, 2 Maccabees 13 having been interpolated by Jason of Cyrene into a prior source.[58] This source for him is DMP, since it would contain a history of persecutions (2 Maccabees 12), the deaths of persecutors (2 Macc 14:1-2), and the death of Nicanor (2 Maccabees 15). Since the death of

---

[57] This position of Goldstein's also blithely accepts the identification of the Hyrcanus, son of Tobias, at 2 Macc 3:11 with the Hyrcanus, grandson of Tobias whose exploits are recounted with relish by Josephus (*Ant* 12.186.236). Such a connection is unfounded and has no textual support. The name is in common. Given the action of the principle of papponymy in naming, however, one could postulate a son of Tobias whose name was Hyrcanus, and who would be a brother to Joseph, father of the Hyrcanus of Josephus. For the working of papponymy, see F. M. Cross, "A Reconstruction of the Judean Restoration," *JBL* 94 (1975) 4-18. Similar name does not necessarily mean same personage.

[58] Goldstein, *1 Maccabees*, 91-92. One should note that Goldstein's source cuts across the distinction between *Ioudas* and *ho Makkabaios* noted by Bunge.

Nicanor is involved with a notion of the inviolability of the temple at Jerusalem, Goldstein finds in this inviolability another characteristic of the source DMP.

Confirmation of his theory is provided for Goldstein by the two sources which he finds in 2 Maccabees 3, one which neglects the temple, the other which stresses the inviolability of the temple. This second source (2 Macc 3:24-25; 29-30) would belong to DMP, the first (3:26-28; 31-36) to Onias IV. Another suggestion of two sources in 2 Maccabees 3 will be discussed below. For the moment, one can see that Goldstein's division does not work on the basic literary level of the text. *Proeirēmenon* is used in one source at 3:28 to refer to *to gazophylakion* which is only mentioned in the other source (3:24). *Doryphorias* at 3:28 picks up the *tois doryphorois* of 3:24 as *dynasteian* of 3:28 does *ho . . . dynastēs* of 3:24, but Goldstein relegates them to different sources. Finally, 3:29-30 are clearly a conclusion to the whole incident, as the condition of Heliodorus is contrasted with the rejoicing of the formerly helpless Jews. In Goldstein's source division, however, there is no description of what happened to Heliodorus prior to this conclusion. One simply has the appearance of the horse and rider before Heliodorus.

Goldstein's source division is not based on an analysis of the text, but on a previous theory. His source DMP is not confirmed. The failure of this "source" theory is best illustrated by Goldstein's classification of the execution of Andonicus (2 Macc 4:34-38). This murderer of Onias III is stripped of his rank by Antiochus IV, led in public disgrace through the city, and then executed on the very same spot where he had struck down Onias III. This death of an impious murderer is not, however, put in the source DMP. Goldstein places it in the history of Onias IV, because Onias IV would have been concerned about the death of his father and would take pleasure in showing how pagans sympathized with a righteous Jew.[59] One can see from this example that Goldstein has no objective literary criteria for determining what belongs to one source or another.

In conclusion, Goldstein has not shown the existence of his source DMP, nor has he demonstrated the existence of a history of the Oniads by Onias IV. Such "sources" are not present in 2 Maccabees.

B. 2. Doublets and Additions

So far I have addressed the question of major sources in 2 Maccabees. Arguments have also been advanced for the presence of doublets in the present text, as well as major additions to the text.

[59] Goldstein, *1 Maccabees*, 102, fn.44.

a) 2 Maccabees 3

I have already discussed the theory of J. A. Goldstein about sources in 2 Maccabees 3. The other main proponent of sources in this section is E. Bickermann, and recently C. Habicht has accepted Bickermann's theory.[60] Bickermann's two sources are 3:24-25; 27-28; 30 (source A) and 3:26.29.31-34 (source B). Bickermann was not the first to propose such a theory, as J. Moffatt had already suggested that the horse/rider did not belong to the account since they did not appear again.[61] H. Bévenot picked up the idea, since such a theory provided two independent accounts which witnessed to the historicity of the event.[62] Bickermann was the first to elaborate the division.

Bickermann bases his division on the fact that Heliodorus is twice said to fall down—3:27.29. According to 3:28, however, Heliodorus is being carried off the scene by his followers (*ederon*), while in 3:29 he is still lying down (*erripto*). The imperfect of 3:28, says Bickermann, is incompatible with the pluperfect of 3:29. Such grammatical incoherence would show that two different accounts of Heliodorus have been combined. Having discerned this duality, Bickermann assigns the verses to one account or the other. Since the followers of Heliodorus are mentioned in 3:25, this verse must belong with 3:24.28 where they are also mentioned. The sudden fall of Heliodorus in 3:27 can only correspond to the onrush of the rearing horse in 3:25, so these two verses belong together. The phrase of 3:30, *epiphanentos kyriou*, belongs with the *epiphaneian* in 3:24. As a description of thanksgiving, 3:30 belongs to the end of account A. As for version B, the two young men who appear in 3:26 appear again in 3:33-34. But 3:33-34 cannot be separated from the preceding 3:31-32 and the following 3:35-36. Chap. 3:29 must also be attached to this complex, since the phrase of 3:26 (*pollas epirriptountes*) is echoed by *erripto* in 3:29, a weak argument. All these arguments are, in fact, secondary to the observation that Heliodorus twice falls, and that he is said to be still lying down after he has been supposed to be carried out.

What, then, of Bickermann's major argument? He has chosen to ignore the fact that 3:29-30 is the conclusion of the epiphany. This conclusion is framed antithetically in a *men . . . de* construction: the voiceless Heliodorus contrasts with the praising crowds, the hopeless Heliodorus with the joyful believers. The pluperfect *erripto* corresponds, even in sentence position, to

---

[60] E. Bickermann, "Héliodore au Temple de Jérusalem," *Annuaire de l'Institut de Philologie et d'Histoire Orientales et Slaves. Bruxelles* 7 (1939-1944) 5-40. C. Habicht, *2 Makkabäerbuch* (JSHRZ 1.3; Gütersloh: G. Mohn, 1976) 172.

[61] J. Moffatt, "2 Maccabees," *APOT* 3. ad loc.

[62] H. Bévenot, *Die beiden Makkabäerbücher. Heilige Schrift des AT* (Bonn: Peter Hanstein, 1931) 4.125.

the pluperfect *epeplērōto.* One cannot separate 3:29 from 3:30 as Bickermann does. Again, as a conclusion to the epiphany, 3:29 is a summation of previous events, and the resumptive pluperfect is to be expected; it is not in conflict with the events of 3:28. With the fall of this argument falls the whole of his thesis.

One fact which remains is that the horse/rider are not mentioned again in the account. This verse is missing from the Latin manuscript tradition, and so P. Katz suggests that it may be a secondary interpolation.[63] If one does retain the verse, there still seems to be no reason to search for two sources behind the acount. In Herodotus' account of the Persian attack on the temple of Delphi (8.36-38), weapons mysteriously appear before the temple of Apollo, but no use is made of them later in the account. It would seem to be another touch to heighten the divine character of the repulse, and no other source should be sought where Apollo would be described as putting on the arms and routing the enemy with them. Similarly, in 2 Maccabees 3, one should treat the appearance of the horse/rider as part of an attempt to paint a vivid attack on Heliodorus, not the remnant of another story but a not unexpected conflation from an author of epiphanies.

b) 2 Macc 6:18-21:

C. Habicht claims that there exist two sources in the account of the martyrdom of Eleazar, an earlier (6:21-28) and a later (6:18-20; 30-31). Only the earlier source would go back to Jason of Cyrene.[64] As evidence for this statement, Habicht cites an article by P. Katz.[65] Katz' article, however, sets out to prove exactly the opposite of what Habicht claims. Katz argues that the story in the present editions of the text is implausible: in these editions, Eleazar is first forced to open his mouth and eat pork, which he spits out; only afterward do his friends suggest a stratagem by which he could avoid eating the pork. Such an ordering of events is illogical. Katz then offers sound text-critical arguments for showing that the text should be changed on the basis of the Latin manuscripts. Katz would read *protupōsas* instead of *proptusas* at 6:20, and *tygchanōn* instead of *anachanōn* at 6:18. With these readings, Katz is convinced that he has restored "a reasonable and convincing progress to the story."[66] Since Habicht himself accepts these readings in his own text, he should accept Katz' conclusion that the story is unified.

[63] P. Katz, "The Text," 19.
[64] Habicht, *2 Makkabäerbuch,* 173.
[65] P. Katz, "Eleazar's Martyrdom in 2 Maccabees: The Latin Evidence for a Point of the Story," *Studia Patristica IV* (ed. F. L. Cross; TU 79; Berlin: Akademie, 1961) 118-124.
[66] Katz, "Eleazar's Martyrdom," 123.

c) 2 Maccabees 7:

C. Habicht has defended the notion that the account of the martyrdom of the mother and her seven sons is an insertion into the story, probably made by a redactor of the epitome.[67] His argument is based on the belief that 2 Macc 7:42 should have originally stood after 2 Macc 6:31. This is so, according to Habicht, because the word *splagchnismos* is never found in 2 Maccabees 7 except at 7:42; but it occurs at 6:7.21 and the verb *splagchnizein* at 6:8.. However, Habicht has overlooked the second half of 7:42: *tas hyperballousas aikias.* The verb *aikizesthai* is found, in 2 Maccabees, only at 7:1.13.15; 8:28.30, and not in 2 Maccabees 6. Clearly 2 Macc 7:42, through its use of both *splagchnismos* and *aikia*, is summarizing the events of 2 Maccabees 6 and 7.

Habicht also argues that 2 Maccabees 7 is later both because Antiochus IV is present at the trial when he should be back in Antioch according to 2 Macc 5:21, and because Semiticisms betray a Hebrew original.[68] I would agree that this popular tale no doubt existed independently; indeed, it was used in Rabbinic materials to apply to later persecutions.[69] However, no one can tell whether Jason or someone else used the story. What one can say is that it fits its present context in the epitome admirably, both through the summary at 2 Macc 7:42 and through the theme of reconciliation through suffering.

Conclusion:

Much of the argumentation in this chapter has been negative, but the thrust of the whole chapter has been positive. For it has shown that the epitome is a unified piece, separate from the prefixed letters and not a

---

[67] Habicht, *2 Makkabäerbuch,* note to 7:1.

[68] For a discussion of Semiticisms affecting syntax, see the following chapter. Besides those discussed there, Habicht also notes the following factors as "ungriechisch." 7:2: *Ti melleis erōtan kai manthanein hēmōn*; While it is difficult to pin down the exact meaning of *mellein* ("to expect," "to wish"), there is nothing Semitic here; *mellein* + pres.inf. is common. 7:6: But this is a quotation from the LXX and its echo. 7:9: The thrice-repeated *hēmas*. But could not this repetition be conscious? Even if not, it may not be correct style, but it is certainly not a Semiticism. 7:9: *eis aiōnion anabiōsin zōēs.* Habicht claims that *aiōnion* should agree with *zōēs*, not *anabiōsin.* However, this is a clear example of hypallage, where a word, instead of agreeing with the case it logically qualifies, is made to agree grammatically with another case. 7:17: *sperma.* But Liddell and Scott list "seed," "offspring" as a perfectly respectable meaning.

[69] For a discussion of these texts, see R. Doran, "The Martyr: A Synoptic View of the Mother and Her Seven Sons," *Ideal Figures in Ancient Judaism: Profiles and Paradigms* (eds. John Collins and G. Nickelsburg; Chico: Scholars Press, 1980) 189-221.

patchwork quilt of sources. This is not to deny that the epitome shows that information was gained from many quarters. The application of the methods of source-criticism, however, has failed to turn up "sources" in the technical sense.

The epitome, therefore, must be considered as a whole and analysed accordingly.

CHAPTER TWO

THE SYNTAX AND STYLE OF 2 MACCABEES

Once one has decided that the narrative of 2 Macc 2:19-15:38 is a separate unit and that it is not a scissors-and-paste use of sources, one can then attempt to analyse its literary character. Before one does this, however, one has first to decide at what level of composition the author of the epitome was working. Was he a careful writer, or nonchalant, or sloppy, or did he simply not have the ability to write well? To answer this question, one has to undertake an analysis of the syntax and style of the narrative of 2 Maccabees.

Previous scholars have concentrated their attention on the rhetorical techniques found in the narrative, to the neglect of the study of syntax. Whether consciously or not, the discussion was limited to these devices because 2 Maccabees was defined as a work belonging to the genre of rhetorical or pathetic historiography.[1] This concentration on the rhetorical features of the work is vividly shown in the recent thesis of W. Richnow.[2] In the main section of his work, entitled "Die sprachliche Form," Richnow spends five pages on syntax, 24 pages on word choice, and 44 pages on rhetorical techniques. More space is devoted to the role of metaphor in 2 Maccabees than to the syntax of the work. This emphasis on rhetoric is found also in the article of L. Gil on the style of the work, an article which is frequently quoted by Richnow.[3] Gil's focus on rhetorics leads him to conclude that 2 Maccabees is written in the style of Asianism, or rather in both styles of Asianism, that of Hegesias and that of the stele of Antiochus of Commagene.[4] To come to such a definite conclusion without an analysis of the syntax seems precipitous.

While I will discuss briefly the rhetorical techniques found in 2 Maccabees, I will first attempt to evaluate its syntax. Since this book is not primarily a dissertation on Hellenistic grammar, I have selected points of grammar which lend themselves to comparison with other writers. Herein lies a major

---

[1] This whole question will be discussed in chapter four.

[2] W. Richnow, "Untersuchungen."

[3] L. Gill, "Sobre el estilo de libro de los Macabeos," *Emérita* 26 (1958) 11-32.

[4] L. Gill, "Sobre el estilo," 30-32; W. Richnow ("Untersuchungen," 190) states that 2 Maccabees is Asianic.

difficulty: what are to be these comparable writings? One can compare the syntax of 2 Maccabees with "classical" Greek (i.e., writers before Alexander), but what of the period after Alexander and before the classicist reaction? From this post-classical but pre-classicist period, the grammar of prose writers such as Polybius and Diodorus Siculus has been well investigated, as well as that of the NT. However, the NT is not a unified book, and it is difficult to speak of *the* grammar of the NT. This difficulty becomes even more acute with corpora of materials such as the papyri and the LXX. Such corpora are indispensable for comparison, even if the only aid to their use remains the grammars such as Mayser for the papyri and Thackeray for the LXX.[5] With the qualification, then, that a thorough classification of the literary level of the various documents in these two corpora remains in the future, I will attempt to bring them into the discussion. In particular, I will compare 2 Maccabees with 3 Maccabees and the Letter of Aristeas. I have also used where relevant the works of Parthenius, Chariton, and Strabo. In the use of Chariton, the work of A. D. Papanikolaou has been especially helpful.[6] Papanikolaou has shown, by his analysis of the syntax of Chariton, that the novel is pre-classicist and dates from the first century C.E. It thus fits our time reference. The prose outline of love stories which Parthenius wrote in the first century B.C.E. also belongs to the period. As for Strabo, I have used 40 pages of Teubner text, chosen at random: 4.1-5. Where possible, I have also made use of the remarks of L. Rydbeck on the technical prose of this period, i.e., the prose written not by littérateurs but by medical men such as Dioscorides.[7] Rydbeck has shown convincingly that their unadorned style and syntax have much in common with those of the NT.

Through comparison with these works, I will attempt to gain a more precise evaluation of the literary ability of the author of the epitome. For the text of 2 Maccabees, I have used as a basis the edition of R. Hanhart, unless otherwise noted.[8]

Orthography and Accidence:

Before analyzing the syntax of the epitome, some facets of orthography and accidence deserve attention.

---

[5]   E. Mayser, *Grammatik der griechischen Papyri aus der Ptolemäerzeit* (Leipzig/Berlin: de Gruyter, 1923-1934); H. St. John Thackeray *A Grammar of the Old Testament in Greek* (Cambridge: Cambridge University Press, 1909).

[6]   A. D. Papanikolaou, *Zur Sprache Charitons* (Cologne: Universität zu Köln, 1963).

[7]   L. Rydbeck, *Fachprosa, vermeintliche Volkssprache und Neues Testament. Zur Beurteilung der sprachlichen Niveauunterschiede im nachklassischen Griechischen.* (Studia Graeca Upsaliensia 5; Stockholm: Almquist & Wiksell, 1967).

[8]   *Maccabaeorum Liber II*, ed. R. Hanhart (Vetus Testamentum Graecum 9/2; Göttingen: Vandenhoeck & Ruprecht, 1959).

The Double Consonants -ττ-, -σσ-.

Attic Greek used the double consonants ττ, while Ionic and most other dialects used σσ.[9] For Polybius, J. A. de Foucault states that the double ττ alternates with the double σσ in words like θάλαττα or τέτταρες.[10] In the papyri, wherever Mayser finds the ττ form, he characterizes it as a survival of Attic and due to the influence of literary models. In the Koine, according to Mayser, the Attic ττ was more and more overshadowed by the Doric-Ionic σσ.[11] Both Thackeray and Moulton recognized that this incursion did not affect some words: derivatives of the Attic ἡττᾶσθαι and ἐλαττοῦν.[12] Forms of ἐλάττων and its antithesis κρείττων both appear in the LXX and NT. However, apart from these three words, ἡττᾶσθαι, ἐλάττων, κρείττων, the σσ form is universal in the LXX. In 3 Maccabees, the σσ is the basic form which appears 10 times, while there is one example of the form ττ (3 Macc 5:37: προστάττειν).[13] The Letter of Aristeas shows a similar preference for forms in σσ : πράσσειν frequently as opposed to one instance of πράττειν (Aristeas 189); ἐπιτάσσειν (Aristeas 94); φυλάσσειν (Aristeas 102.311); δια-φυλάσσειν (Aristeas 272); but ἐκπλήττεσθαι (Aristeas 196).[14] In Parthenius, R. Mayer-G'Schrey comments: "σσ et ττ promiscue extant."[15]

In 2 Maccabees, the ττ forms occur with the derivatives ἥττων and ἐλάττων.[16] They are also found in πράττειν and φρυάττειν.[17] Both διαφυ-λάττειν and διαφυλάσσειν are found,[18] as well as τάττειν, ἐπιτάσσειν and

⁹ H. W. Smyth, *Greek Grammar* (Cambridge: Harvard University Press, 1971) 78.

¹⁰ J. A. de Foucault, *Recherches sur la Langue et le Style de Polybe* (Paris: Société d'édition "Les belles Lettres," 1972) 63.

¹¹ E. Mayser, *Grammatik*, 1. 233.

¹² Thackeray, *A Grammar*, 121-122; J. H. Moulton and W. F. Howard, *A Grammar of New Testament Greek, Vol II* (Edinburgh: T. & T. Clark, 1976) 107.

¹³ In the manuscript tradition, there is slight variation. At 3 Macc 2:29, 671 reads ττ; at 2:32, 370 and 534 read ττ; at 3:3, 52 reads ττ; and at 7:20, 62 reads θάλαττης. Cf. *Maccabaeorum Liber III*, ed. R Hanhart. (Vetus Testamentum Graecum 9/3; Göttingen: Vandenhoeck & Ruprecht, 1960) 35.

¹⁴ H. G. Meecham, *The Letter of Aristeas. A Linguistic Study with special Reference to the Greek Bible* (Manchester: Manchester University Press, 1935) 82.

¹⁵ R. Mayer-G'Schrey, *Parthenius Nicaeensis quale in Fabularum Amatoriarum Breviario dicendi genus secutus sit* (Heidelberg: C. Winter, 1898) 4. In referring to the work of Parthenius, I have followed a double system. The first set of letters refers to the LCL edition. E.G., 1.2 refers to the first love story of Parthenius, the second paragraph. The set of numbers in brackets refers to the page and line in the edition of P. Sakolowski (Leipzig: Teubner, 1896).

¹⁶ ἥττων: 4:40; 5:14; 10:17; 13:23; 15:18.27. ἐλάττων: 5:5; 8:9; 10:18; 12:4(74 reads ἐλάσσονας).10. ἐλάττωμα: 11:13. ἐλαττονοῦν: 12:11; 13:19.

¹⁷ πράττειν: 9:19; 12:43 (L'-⁶² read πράσσων); 14:23. ἀντιπράττειν: 14:29. φρυάττειν: 7:34.

¹⁸ διαφυλάττειν: 6:6 (311 reads διαφυλάσσειν); 10:30 (A reads διεφύλασσον). διαφυ-λάσσειν: 3:22 (46-52 read διαφυλάττειν).

προστάσσειν.[19] The σσ forms occur with ταράσσειν, θάλασσα and μεταλλάσσειν.[20] In sum, then, one does find a high proportion of ττ forms in 2 Maccabees, as in Polybius and Parthenius, and so the author of 2 Maccabees must remain under the influence of Attic literary models.

Word Declension:

The declension of the word for "temple" is informative. The Attic form is νεώς, but, after 250 B.C.E., the Dorian form ναός becomes prevalent.[21] In Polybius, one finds both ναός (4.18.10; 16.25.7) and νεώς (4.35.1; 15.29.8; 16.6.2-3)—at 16.1.5, one finds τοὺς νεώς close by ναούς at 16.1.6. In Diodorus Siculus, τοῦ νεώ is present at 4.83.1, but ναούς at 1.15.3-5; 20.14.3. Ναός is always found in the LXX and NT, as in 3 Maccabees. Strabo uses "temple" twice in 4.1-5, and he uses νεώς (4.1.4; 4.1.11). Parthenius uses "temple" once, and there he uses ναός (1.2 [6,14]).

In 2 Maccabees, the forms of νεώς and ναός are evenly divided: νεώς at 4:14; 6:2; 9:16; 10:3.5; 13:23; 14:33; ναός at 8:2; 10:5; 14:35; 15:18.33.[22] In this respect, then, the author of 2 Maccabees retains some traces of the Attic form, similar to Polybius and Diodorus Siculus.

Numbers:

In classical usage, numbers are added together by placing the smaller number before the larger and joining them by καί (or τε καί), or by placing the smaller after the larger with or without καί: πέντε καὶ εἴκοσι(ν) or εἴκοσι (καὶ) πέντε. However, one sometimes finds numbers added through the preposition ἐπί or, less often, πρός with the dative. Kühner-Blass state that this mode of expression, through the preposition ἐπί or more seldom πρός with the dative, is found among later authors as, for example, Plutarch (*Publicola* 20.1: τρισχιλίους ἐπὶ μυρίοις = 13,000) and Diodorus Siculus (16.53.1: Ὀλυμπιὰς . . . ὀγδόη πρὸς ταῖς ἑκατόν = on the 108th Olympiad).[23] They note that such a mode of expression was regular, however, on

---

[19] τάττειν: 10:28. ἐπιτάσσειν: 9:8. προστάσσειν: 15:5.

[20] ταράσσειν: 9:24 (58 711 read ἐπιταράττωνται); 14:19 (V 347 read ταραττομένοις). θάλασσα: 9:8. μεταλλάσσειν: 7:14. Cf. also γλωσσοτομεῖν: 7:4 (V 55 read γλωττοτομεῖν). γλῶσσαν: 7:10 (L'-236 55 read γλῶτταν); 15:33. ἐκπλήσσεσθαι: 7:12 (534-62 55 read ἐκπλήττεσθαι). περισσός: 12:44 (L' 311 read περιττόν).

[21] E. Mayser, *Grammatik*, 1.260.

[22] At 4:14, L reads ναοῦ; at 6:2, 381-534 56 106 Tht.ᴮ read ναόν; at 14:33, 381 reads ναόν. At 8:2, 1 reads νεώς; at 10:5, L' reads νεώ.

[23] R. Kühner-F. Blass, *Ausführliche Grammatik der griechischen Sprache* (Hanover: Hahn, 1890), 1.630.

Attic inscriptions to give the date from the number 13 to 19. Mayser does not discuss the use of prepositions to form numbers; only in his discussion of the dating of days of the month are examples found where ἐπί is used: πέμπηι ἐπ᾽ εἰκάδι.[24] In the LXX and NT, this mode of expressing numbers is not found, outside of 2 Maccabees.[25]

This only brings into sharper light the similarity between the usage of Polybius and that of the author of 2 Maccabees. In Polybius, numbers are expressed more frequently by prepositions than by the conjunction καί. Πρός is found often, but also σύν and ἐπί.[26] In 2 Maccabees, πρός with the dative is found nine times: 4:8.9; 5:21.24; 8:22; 10:31; 11:11 bis; 12:20.

Conjugation:

In 2 Maccabees, the pluperfect tense always has the syllabic augment as in classical usage. This is in contrast to the LXX and the NT, where the augment in the pluperfect tended to disappear, particularly in the active forms, less so in the passive. At 3 Macc 1:1, the augment is missing from παρεμβεβλήκεισαν. In Parthenius, the augment is missing from ἐπιλελοίπει at 6.3 (13,16), although Sakolowski has emended the text to ἐπελελοίπει. "In Polybius, the augment greatly preponderates in simplicia, though often dropped in compounds, especially in active forms."[27] The constancy of 2 Maccabees' usage amidst this fluctuation stands clearer.

Two forms are of note. Hanhart has given the reading of the uncials at 2 Macc 14:5 and 10:21, and he read καθέστηκαν and πέπρακαν respectively.[28] Here the 3rd person plural ending of the perfect -ασι has been replaced by the aorist ending -αν. This phenomenon is common in inscriptions from the 3rd century B.C.E. on. While Sextus Empiricus characterized it as Alexandrian (*Adv Gramm* 213), it is a common feature of Hellenistic Greek, and has been found in inscriptions from Pergamum.[29] It is well attested in the NT and in LXX.[30]

Secondly, Hanhart wishes to retain the sigmatic aorist at 2 Macc 15:7

---

[24] Mayser, *Grammatik*, I.2.

[25] Thackeray, *A Grammar*, 188.

[26] J. A. de Foucault, *Recherches*, 67.

[27] Moulton and Howard, *A Grammar, Vol. II*, 190.

[28] 14:5: V 55 771 καθέστηκαν; A -κεν; 106 -κεσαν; the rest read -κασιν. 10:21: πέπρακαν A′ V 55 347 771; πεπράκασι(ν) q 381-1 46-52 58 311; πεπράκοσι(ν) L⁻³⁸¹.

[29] See B. G. Mandilaras, *Studies in the Greek Language* (Athens: N. Xenopoulos Press, 1972) 13-14.

[30] Moulton and Howard, *A Grammar*, 2.221.

and 3 Macc 2:33: τεύξασθαι. However, the change from -ξεσθαι to -ξασθαι can be seen as a scribal blunder, of which there are several similar cases.[31]

Syntax:

Demonstratives.

῞Οδε. In classical Greek, ὅδε points with emphasis to an object in the immediate (actual or mental) vicinity of the speaker, or to something just noticed. Οὗτος may refer to a person close at hand, but less vividly. Οὗτος generally refers to what precedes, ὅδε (τοιόσδε) to what follows.[32]

Polybius uses οὗτος and ὅδε without distinguishing them.[33] In Diodorus Siculus, -δε forms are mainly found in mechanical phrases: ἡ κατασκευὴ τοιάδε; τόνδε τὸν τρόπον; ἐπὶ τοῖσδε + inf.; τὴν ἐπιστολὴν τήνδε; μέχρι τῶνδε τῶν χρόνων (καιρῶν); τῶνδε τῶν ἱστοριῶν; τήνδε τὴν βίβλον.[34] In Parthenius, ὅδε is frequent[35] and refers to what went before, e.g., 3.3 (9,11); 7.2 (15,13).

῞Οδε is lacking in 1st century B.C.E. papyri,[36] and is found in the NT and LXX mostly in the formula τάδε λέγει (Acts 21:11; Rev 2:1). Thackeray holds that in some cases it is used as equal to οὗτος.[37]

There are seven instances of -δε in the narrative of 2 Maccabees. In all these instances, the forms are used as in classical Greek. At 2 Macc 15:12 (ἦν δὲ ἡ τούτου θεωρία τοιάδε) and 15:22 (ἔλεγε δὲ ἐπικαλούμενος τόνδε τὸν τρόπον), ὅδε refers to what follows. At 2 Macc 6:12 (τοὺς ἐντυγχάνοντας τῆδε τῇ βίβλῳ), 14:33 (τόνδε τὸν τοῦ θεοῦ σηκόν), and 14:36 (τόνδε τόν προσφάτως κεκαθαρισμένον οἶκον), the reference is emphatically to an object in the immediate vicinity of the speaker. At 2 Macc 10:8 (κατ'ἐνιαυτὸν ἄγειν τάσδε τὰς ἡμέρας) and 15:36 (μηδαμῶς ἐᾶσαι ἀπαρασήμαντον τήνδε τὴν ἡμέραν), the reference is again made, with emphasis, to what is mentally present to the speaker. This attention to classical usage in 2 Maccabees is striking.

[31] P. Katz, "The Text of 2 Maccabees Reconsidered," *ZNW* 51 (1960) 22. Cf. Jos *Ant* 12.115; 15.342.

[32] H. W. Smyth, *Greek Grammar*, 1241.1245.

[33] F. Kaelker, "Quaestiones de elocutione Polybiana," *Leipziger Studien zur classischen Philologie, III* (Leipzig: Hirzel, 1880) 277.

[34] J. Palm, *Über Sprache und Stil des Diodoros von Sizilien* (Lund: CWK Gleerup, 1955) 74.

[35] R. Mayer-G'Schrey, *Parthenius*, 42-43.

[36] Mayser, *Grammatik*, 2.1.73.

[37] Thackeray, *The Grammar*, 191.

The Tenses:

a) Perfect. In classical usage, the perfect denotes a completed action the effects of which still continue in the present. If this is not so, the aorist tense is used.[38] In the Hellenistic period, P. Chantraine has shown that the perfect tense was increasingly used with the sense of the aorist.[39] Mayser has documented this phenomenon in the papyri, where both tenses were, at times, used promiscuously.[40] The aoristic perfect is also found in Polybius, particularly in formulas where Polybius refers to earlier portions of his work: 3.10.1: καθάπερ ἐν ταῖς πρὸ ταύτης βύβλοις . . . δεδηλώκαμεν, but, in contrast, 3.48.6: καθάπερ ἡμεῖς ἐν τοῖς πρὸ τουτῶν ἐδηλώσαμεν. The aoristic perfect is also found at 1.17.11 (ἡ τῶν ἐθισμῶν διαφορὰ καὶ τότε καὶ πολλάκις ἤδη σέσωκε τὰ Ῥωμαίων πράγματα) among others.[41] N. Turner has documented its use in the NT and also in the LXX.[42] It is present in the Letter of Aristeas (173: φιλοφρόνως ἠσπασάμεθα τὸν βασιλέα καὶ τὰς ἐπιστολὰς ἀποδεδώκαμεν). Papanikolaou has also shown that it is present in Chariton's romance: 1.5.5: χείρονα δέδρακα ἱεροσύλων . . . "I have committed a crime worse than temple-robbing."[43]

What of the usage in 2 Maccabees? I have found no trace of this aoristic perfect in 2 Maccabees. The perfect retains the sense of resultant action. This is so at 2 Macc 3:33 (διὰ γὰρ αὐτόν σοι κεχάρισται τὸ ζῆν ὁ κύριος); 7:11.33.35; 8:18; 14:7. This is true also of those perfects which are found in reports of direct speech: 10:21: ὡς ἀργυρίου πέπρακαν τοὺς ἀδελφούς; 14:5: ἐν τίνι διαθέσει καὶ βουλῇ καθέστηκαν οἱ Ἰουδαῖοι. The perfect is used in 2 Maccabees to reproduce the thoughts of others. For example, at 2 Macc 14:31, one reads: ὅτι γενναίως ὑπὸ τἀνδρὸς ἐστρατήγημαι. Here, the perfect reports the thought of Nicanor, "I have been out-maneuvered by the fellow." The same could be said of the perfect at 2 Macc 5:17, which reports that Antiochus IV did not know that the Lord was angry (ἀπώργισται) and that therefore there was neglect (διὸ γέγονε . . . παρόρασις) of the temple—a present state brought about by a past action. At 2 Macc 9:24 (ᾧ

[38] R. Kühner-B. Gerth, *Ausführliche Grammatik der griechischen Sprache* (Hanover/Leipzig: Hahn, 1898-1904) 1.167.

[39] P. Chantraine, *Histoire du Parfait Grec* (Paris: H. Champion, 1927).

[40] Mayser, *Grammatik*, 2.1.139-141.

[41] J. A. de Foucault, *Recherches*, 134-137.

[42] J. H. Moulton and N. Turner, *A Grammar of New Testament Greek* (Edinburgh: T. & T. Clark, 1963) 3.68.71.

[43] For a full listing, see Papanikolaou, *Zur Sprache*, 51-53.

καταλέλειπται τὰ πράγματα), the thought of the surrounding chieftains is given—they know to whom the rule has been bequeathed, and that bequest still holds good. The perfect tense is also found in letters, and these are examples of what Smyth calls "epistolary tenses."[44] Here the writer of a letter puts himself in the position of the reader who views the action as past. Such perfects are found at 2 Macc 9:25 (ἀναδέδειχα τὸν υἱόν . . . γέγραφα); 9:27 (πέπεισμαι); 11:20 (ἐντέταλμαι); 11:32 (πέπομφα). There are numerous examples in the papyri to parallel those in 2 Maccabees, particularly in the use of γέγραφα, πέπομφα, ἐντέταλμαι.[45]

In 2 Maccabees, the perfect is used to denote a past action whose effects still continue in the present.

b) Future.

In classical Greek, when the context shows that stress is laid on the idea of futurity, the future infinitive, referring to future time relative to the main verb, is sometimes used instead of the present or aorist. Πολλοῦ δέω ἐμαυτόν γε ἀδικήσειν καὶ κατ᾽ ἐμαυτοῦ ἐρεῖν "I am far from intending to harm myself and to speak to my own disadvantage" (Plato *Apology* 37B). Verbs signifying "to hope, expect, promise, swear" and some others of like meaning take either the future infinitive (in indirect discourse), or the aorist, less often the present, infinitive (not in indirect discourse).[46] Ἐν ἐλπίδι ὢν καὶ τὰ τείχη τῶν Ἀθηναίων αἱρήσειν "Hoping that he would capture the walls of the Athenians" (*Th* 7.46); ὑπέσχετο ταῦτα ποιήσειν "he promised that he would do this" (*Lys* 12.14).

In the papyri, verbs of hoping, expectation, promise, etc., take the future infinitive, but the examples in Mayser are nearly all early.[47] In the LXX, "the infinitive and participle of the future are not often met with outside literary books."[48] By the time of the NT, the future infinitive "has died out of colloquial speech, . . . but it is still found in *Acts* and *Hebrews*."[49]

In Polybius, J. A. de Faucault noticed a growing confusion between the future and aorist infinitives. He agrees with V. Magnien that the future infinitive is no longer a living form and that it was not used correctly.[50] In Parthenius, the aorist infinitive is used instead of the future at 5.2 (11,15): οἰόμενος ῥᾷστα ἀπαλλάξασθαι τῆς νόσου "thinking that he would easily be

44 Smyth, *Greek Grammar*, 1942.
45 Mayser, *Grammatik*, 2.1.183.
46 Smyth, *Greek Grammar*, 1868.
47 Mayser, *Grammatik*, 2.1.216.
48 Thackeray, *A Grammar*, 194.
49 Moulton and Turner, *A Grammar*, 3.86.
50 J. A. de Foucault, *Recherches*, 159.

rid of his trouble"; 17.4 (32,23): εἰ αὖτις λέγοι αὐτὴν παρ' αὐτὸν ἀφικέσθαι "if he would like the woman to come again." In 3 Maccabees, the future infinitive is used twice, once after a verb of promising: 3 Macc 1:4: ἐπαγγελλομένη δώσειν νικήσασιν ἑκάστῳ δύο μνᾶς χρυσίου "promising to give each man, if they were victorious, two minae of gold"; 1:26: τέλος ἐπιθήσειν δοκῶν τῷ προειρημένῳ "thinking to put an end to his intention." In 2 Maccabees, the future infinitive is found after verbs of expectation, hope, swearing, and promising (2 Macc 7:14; 7:24; 8:11; 9:22; 12:11). At 2 Macc 4:9, ὑπισχνέομαι is used with a present infinitive: καὶ ἕτερα διαγράφειν. Here the meaning would seem to be "to pledge that he would pay more"; such a meaning of ὑπισχνέομαι with the present infinitive is found in classical authors: Xen An 7.7.31: ἐὰν μὲν οἱ στρατιῶται ὑπισχνῶνται προθυμότερον αὐτοῖς συστρατεύεσθαι, ἄν τὰ παρὰ σοῦ νῦν ἀναπράξωσιν "if the soldiers pledge to render them (such leaders) more zealous service if they now exact what you owe."[Editors emend to συστρατεύσεσθαι without reason.] The future infinitive is found in 2 Maccabees after verbs of saying or thinking in indirect discourse, as at 7:19: σὺ δὲ μὴ νομίσῃς ἀθῷος ἔσεσθαι θεομαχεῖν ἐπιχειρήσας "Do not think that you will be guiltless, since you have attempted to fight God." At 7:26, the future infinitive refers to an action after the action of the main verb: ἐπεδέξατο πείσειν τὸν υἱόν "she agreed to persuade her son."

However, there is confusion between the future and the aorist infinitive in 2 Maccabees. For example, at 2 Macc 9:8, ὁ δ' ἄρτι δοκῶν τοῖς τῆς θαλάσσης κύμασιν ἐπιτάσσειν διὰ τὴν ὑπὲρ ἄνθρωπον ἀλαζονείαν καὶ πλάστιγγι τὰ τῶν ὀρέων οἰόμενος ὕψη στήσειν. Here there is no reason why the present infinitive should have been used after δοκῶν, while the future after οἰόμενος. Οἴομαι is used with the future infinitive at 13:3, but with the aorist infinitive at 5:21 and 9:4. Δοκέω is used with the future infinitive at 14:14. At 9:15 and 15:33, the aorist and future infinitive run in tandem (9:15:οὕτως λέγων τὴν μὲν ἁγίαν πόλιν . . . ἐλευθέραν ἀναδεῖξαι, τοὺς δὲ Ἰουδαίους . . . πάντας αὐτοὺς ἴσους . . . ποιήσειν . . . κοσμήσειν . . . ἀποδώσειν . . . χορηγήσειν; 15:33: ἔφη κατὰ μέρος δώσειν τοῖς ὀρνέοις, τὰ δ' ἐπίχειρα τῆς ἀνοίας κατέναντι τοῦ ναοῦ κρεμάσαι.

The future infinitive, then, is used widely in 2 Maccabees, but it exhibits the same tendency as found in Polybius to be confused with the aorist infinitive.

As for the future participle, it is used in classical Greek to express purpose. V. Magnien comments that Polybius uses it frequently, but that that fact can be attributed to the literary character of his work.[51] The future

51 V. Magnien, Le Futur Grec (Paris: H. Champion, 1912) 2.6.

participle is not frequent in the papyri,[52] and almost absent from the LXX outside "literary works."[53] In the NT, it is virtually limited to Acts: "the present infinitive is occasionally used in its place, and elsewhere the infinitive, a relative clause, or some other phrase."[54] Such use of the future participle to express purpose is found in 3 Macc 1:8; 2:31 and in the Letter of Aristeas 40. Parthenius uses the construction 4 times: 1.2 (6,12); 4.5 (10,18); 8.5 (17,10); 13.2 (25,20).

In 2 Maccabees, the future participle is used predicatively six times with a meaning of purpose, and once after a verb of perception (4:6). The instances of purpose are: 3:14: εἰσῄει τὴν περὶ τούτων ἐπίσκεψιν οἰκονομήσων; 5:9: ἀναχθεὶς ὡς διὰ τὴν συγγένειαν τευξόμενος σκέπης; 10:24: παρῆν ὡς δοριάλωτον λημψόμενος τὴν Ἰουδαίαν; 11:32: πέπομφα δὲ καὶ τὸν Μενέλαον παρακαλέσοντα ὑμᾶς; 12:7: τοῦ δὲ χωρίου συγκλεισθέντος ἀνέλυσε πάλιν ἥξων . . . "But, as soon as the town shut its gates on him, he retired, meaning to come back to exterminate the whole community of Joppa." The final instance is at 4:23: ἀπέστειλεν Ἰάσων Μενέλαον . . . παρακομίζοντα τὰ χρήματα τῷ βασιλεῖ καὶ περὶ πραγμάτων ἀναγκαίων ὑπομνηματισμοὺς τελέσοντα. The distinction between the two participles is intentional—Menelaus was carrying the money to the king, but his mission was to complete the necessary business. Instead of carrying out that mission, Menelaus gained the king's favor and ousted Jason from the ruling position (4:24).

The use of the future participle in 2 Maccabees is evidence of its literary stylization.

The Verbal Adjective -τέος

The use of the verbal adjective -τέος decreases in the Hellenistic period. It occurs once in the NT (Lk 5:38: βλητέον). It is found in the papyri, but infrequently, so that Mayser claims that it never belonged to the living speech but to the literary language and to official documents.[55] Palm holds that the form in -τέος is not unusual in Polybius and Diodorus Siculus; both have the impersonal construction, usually without ἐστί. Diodorus Siculus uses it especially in his main introduction, and thus shows that he holds it to betray a literary style.[56]

---

52 Mayser, *Grammatik*, 2.1.220-223.
53 Thackeray, *A Grammar*, 194.
54 F. Blass, A. Debrunner, R. W. Funk, *A Greek Grammar of the New Testament and other Early Christian Literature* (Chicago: University of Chicago Press, 1961) 351.
55 Mayser, *Grammatik*, 2.1.359-360.
56 J. Palm, *Über Sprache*, 91.

There are no examples of the verbal adjective in 3 Maccabees, and one usage in the Letter of Aristeas 55 (διόπερ οὐ παραβατέον οὐδὲ ὑπερθετέον). Thackeray notes that the verbal adjective is found 5 times in the literary Greek of the Epistle of Jeremiah (39,56: νομιστέον; 39: κλητέον; 51: γνωστέον; 56: ἐκδεκτέον). In 2 Maccabees, the verbal adjective occurs five times, three within the proemium: 2:29: φρονιστέον, ἐξεταστέον; 2:31: συγχωρητέον; 6:17: ἐλευστέον; and once in the impersonal construction with εἶναι: 3:13: ἀναλημπτέα ταῦτα εἶναι. This again shows the literary striving of the author of 2 Maccabees.

Semiticisms:

Εἰ

It has often been thought that εἰ introduces a direct question at 2 Macc 7:7 and 15:3.[57] As such, it would belong to biblical Greek usage, "probably a Hebraism from ־ה or אם, which may also stand in both direct and indirect questions."[58]

However, the usage at 2 Macc 15:3 would seem to be that of an indirect question as at 2 Macc 3:9.

> 3:9: ἐπυνθάνετο δέ, εἰ ταῖς ἀληθείαις ταῦτα οὕτως ἔχοντα τυγχάνει "He asked whether this was really true."
>
> 15:3: ἐπηρώτησεν, εἰ ἔστιν ἐν οὐρανῷ ὁ δυνάστης ὁ προστεταχὼς ἄγειν τὴν τῶν σαββάτων ἡμέραν "He asked if there was a sovereign in heaven who had commanded them to keep the Sabbath."

The use of εἰ to introduce indirect questions is found in classical Greek: Th 1.5.1 ἐρωτῶντες εἰ λῃσταί εἰσιν "asking whether they are pirates."

The situation is somewhat different at 2 Macc 7:7: ἐπηρώτων εἰ φάγεσαι πρὸ τοῦ τιμωρηθῆναι τὸ σῶμα κατὰ μέλος. Both Abel and Habicht seem to understand πρό as "before" (avant que, ehe). However, πρό can mean "rather than" as at Hdt 7.152.3: πᾶν δὴ βουλόμενοι σφίσι εἶναι πρὸ τῆς παρεούσης λύπης "They felt that anything would be better than their present sufferings." (Cf. Liddell and Scott, πρό III.1.) Such a meaning would make perfect sense in the context: the martyr is asked, "Will you eat rather than have your body punished limb by limb?" As such, εἰ would here be introducing an alternative question. However, there are examples in classical Greek where εἰ does introduce such a direct, alternative question. Plato, *Alcibiades I*, 115 A: Εἴ τις ἤδη σοι ἔδοξεν αἰσχρὰ μέν, δίκαια δὲ πράττειν; "Can someone, in your opinion, do what is just, and yet it be shameful?" In

---

57 Moulton and Turner, *A Grammar*, 3.333.
58 Moulton and Turner, *A Grammar*, 3.333.

this case, Socrates is responding to a request for clarification of an earlier question. In *Alcibiades I*, the questioner asks: "What is your question?" As Kühner-Gerth note, this direct question of Socrates to a certain extent depends on an assumed verb. Kühner-Gerth therefore hold that in such cases εἰ should be considered as in an indirect question.[59] However, one can see that 2 Macc 7:7 is not so convincing an example of a Semiticism as Acts 1:6: ἠρώτων αὐτὸν λέγοντες, Κύριε, εἰ ἐν τῷ χρόνῳ τούτῳ ἀποκαθιστάνεις τὴν βασιλείαν τῷ Ἰσραήλ. As an alternative question, 2 Macc 7:7 could derive from the classical use of εἰ in indirect questions.

Ἀποκριθεὶς εἰπεῖν

In the reported vision of Judas at 2 Macc 15:11b-16, Judas first sees Onias, the revered high-priest, and then another venerable person comes into view who is not identified. Onias reveals who the person is, the prophet Jeremiah. The text reads: ἀποκριθέντα δὲ τὸν Ὀνίαν εἰπεῖν. Is this a Semiticism? Turner already suggested that, in itself, the pleonastic use of the participle was not a Semiticism, as it is found in classical Greek (Hdt: ἔφη λέγων, εἰρώτα λέγων, ἔλεγε φάς) and in the papyri. As Turner comments: "There is no doubt, however, that such expressions when used on a large scale, as in biblical Greek, point away from the popular language to a specialized Semitic background."[60] Of particular note is the use in Plato *Protagoras* 314 D: καὶ ἡμεῖς πάλιν ἐκρούμεν, καὶ ὅς ἐγκεκλημένης τῆς θύρας ἀποκρινόμενος εἶπεν, Ὦ ἄνθρωποι, ἔφη, οὐκ ἀκηκόατε "We tried knocking again, and then he spoke in answer through the closed doors, 'Sirs,' he said, 'have you not heard. . . .'" Here the answer of the doorkeeper is to the knocking, not to any express question. One could argue that the same is true in 2 Macc 15:14. Onias is answering, not an expressed question of Judas, but puzzlement surrounding the unknown arrival. The same would be true of the angel's address to the women at the tomb when the guards fall in a swoon: their frightened consternation at the events is answered by the angel (Mt 28:5). This is quite a different case from instances where a pericope begins with Καὶ ἀποκριθεὶς ὁ Ἰησοῦς ἔλεγεν, as at Mk 12:35.

This isolated phrase, then, is not by itself a Semiticism in 2 Macc 15:14.

As noted in our previous chapter, Habicht attempted to separate 2 Maccabees 7 from the rest of the narrative. As part of his discussion, he laid particular emphasis on Semiticisms which occur in this chapter (although he did not discuss the particle εἰ in 2 Macc 7:7). Since I argued above that 2 Maccabees 7 should not be so separated but that it could derive from traditional sources, my case does not rest on showing that there are no

---

[59] Kühner-Gerth, *Ausführliche Grammatik*, 533-534, especially Anm.14.
[60] Moulton and Turner, *A Grammar*, 3.155-156.

Semiticisms in this chapter. However, some of Habicht's Semiticisms are questionable. For example, at 2 Macc 7:2, he finds the use of ἕτοιμοι ... ἤ rather than the comparative ἑτοιμότερος or ἕτοιμοι ... μᾶλλον ἤ "ungriechisch." If this is so, Habicht should also have noted that the same phenomenon occurs at 2 Macc 14:42: εὐγενῶς θέλων ἀποθανεῖν ἤπερ τοῖς ἀλιτηρίοις ὑποχείριος γενέσθαι. One has to note that in these cases it is a question of desire or choice. Kühner-Gerth note that sometimes the comparative ἤ occurs after a positive adjective or after a verb without μᾶλλον, particularly in cases of desire, choice, etc., which contain in themselves the notion of preference and distinction.[61] For example, Homer *Il.* A, 117: βούλομ᾽ ἐγὼ λαὸν σόον ἔμμεναι ἤ ἀπολέσθαι "I myself desire that my people be safe, not perish"; Lysias 2,62: θάνατον μετ᾽ ἐλευθερίας αἱρούμενοι ἤ βίον μετὰ δουλείας "preferring death with freedom rather than life with servitude." In both the examples from 2 Maccabees the element of will and choice is present, and one should not label them as Semiticisms.

Habicht has also called the usage at 2 Macc 7:1 "ungriechisch": ἀπὸ τῶν ... κρεῶν ἐφάπτεσθαι. Here ἀπό is used instead of the simple genitive, and the preposition prefixed to the verb differs from the following preposition. However, as Howard notes the partitive use of ἀπό after ἐσθίειν at Mk 7:28 = Mt 15:27, this "is an instance of the more general use of ἀπό or ἐκ c. gen. to replace the partitive genitive in later Greek."[62] This use of ἀπό to replace the partitive genitive also explains the difference in prepositions, but one should also note that it is not "ungriechisch" for the prefixed preposition to differ: Parthenius has three examples: 15.1 (29,16) ἐπιφοιτῶσα εἰς τὰ λοιπὰ ... ὄρη; 17.4 (32,20) εἰσέρχεται παρὰ τὸν παῖδα; 17.5 (33,6) εἰς πολὺν πόθον ἐπαγάγοιτο. The other examples that Habicht adduces for Semiticisms are not syntactical, but involve word choice; for example, the use of σπέρμα in 2 Macc 7:17 to denote descendents. These were discussed in the previous chapter, footnote 68.

Negation:

Blass-Debrunner-Funk sum up the history of the negatives in this way: "The distinction between the two negatives, objective οὐ and subjective μή, is in part fairly complicated in classical Greek. On the other hand, essentially everything can be subsumed under one rule for the Koine of the NT: οὐ negates the indicative, μή the remaining moods including the infinitive and the participle."[63] First I will discuss the negatives in main and subordinate clauses, then the negatives with the infinitive and the participle.

---

[61] Kühner-Gerth, *Ausführliche Grammatik*, 2.303.
[62] Moulton and Howard, *A Grammar*, 2.461.
[63] Blass-Debrunner-Funk, *A Greek Grammar*, 426.

(i) Negatives in main and subordinate clauses.

As in classical and NT usage, individual words or phrases are always negated by οὐ: 2 Macc 3:14; 4:13.17; 5:5; 6:1; 8:6.9; 11:13; 14:8.30; 15:19.

In the papyri, Mayser has noticed that the boundaries between οὐ and μή in main and subordinate clauses are not so clearly recognized as in classical Greek.[64] Birke suggests that Strabo also is careless in this regard: at 1.2.1 (ἀλλὰ τοὺς μὲν πολλοὺς ἐᾶν, οἷς μηδὲ ἀκολουθεῖν ἄξιον "to leave out of consideration many whom it is not proper to follow") οὐ should be read instead of μή.[65] Within 2 Maccabees, οὐ and μή are used according to classical norms. Ὀυ negates simple statements as well as the indicative in dependent statements (14:3; 15:21) and causal clauses (14:29). Μή negates the subjunctive (3:32; 6:15; 7:19.29; 9:24; 14:22; 15:2), the imperative (7:16.18.34), and conditional clauses (5:18; 12:44; 14:33). Μή is also found at 12:14 in a relative clause: λαλοῦντες, ἃ μὴ θέμις. "Clauses with a relative pronoun referring to an antecedent thought of in respect of its *character* (*of such a sort*) take μή."[66] Similar examples are found not only in the NT (Ti 1:11 διδάσκοντες ἃ μὴ δεῖ), but also in Polybius and Dionysius of Halicarnassus.[67] D. H. 4.82.1: ὑπέμεινεν ὅσα μὴ θέμις ἐλευθέρᾳ γυναικὶ παθεῖν "She endured what it is not legal for a free woman to suffer."

(ii) Negatives with the Infinitive.

In the papyri and the NT, μή is predominant but it is simplifying too much to say that it stands throughout.[68] Since, in classical Greek, the infinitive not in indirect discourse takes μή, while the infinitive in indirect discourse takes οὐ, but sometimes μή,[69] the growth of μή in all uses of the infinitive is not unexpected. In Polybius, verbs of thinking often take both negatives, and οὐ and μή are found with the infinitive in indirect discourse.[70] An example of the confusion can be seen with δεῖν: at 2.26.6, it takes μή (ἔφη δεῖν μή + inf.); at 2.56.10, it takes οὐ (δεῖ τοιγαροῦν οὐκ + inf.); Ὀυ is found with the infinitive in Parthenius,[71] and μή is used instead of οὐ with the infinitive in indirect speech at 18.1 (34,7); 22.2 (38,14); 30.1 (44,15).

In 2 Maccabees, μή negates ὥστε + inf. (4:14; 3:6), the infinitive not in

---

[64] Mayser, *Grammatik*, 2.2/2.550.

[65] O. Birke, *De particularum μή et οὐ usu Polybiano Dionysiaco Diodoreo Strabiano* (Leipzig: O. Schmidt, 1897) 16-24.

[66] Smyth, *Greek Grammar*, 2705g. Blass-Debrunner-Funk (*A Greek Grammar*, 428.4) seem to dispute that this is classical usage.

[67] O. Birke, *De Particularum*, 16-24.

[68] Moulton and Turner, *A Grammar*, 3.285.

[69] Smyth, *Greek Grammar*, 2711.

[70] J. A. de Foucault, *Recherches*, 198-199.

[71] R. Mayer-G'Schrey, *Parthenius*, 52.

indirect discourse (4:19; 6:1.12; 8:16bis; 9:12; 10:4; 13:11; 15:8.36), and the articular infinitive (4:19; 6:13). There are two instances where the infinitive in indirect discourse is negated: 3:11 and 14:32. At 3:11, οὐ is used in accordance with classical rules.[72] 2 Macc 14:32 reads: τῶν δὲ μεθ' ὅρκων φασκόντων μὴ γινώσκειν. Here the statement in indirect discourse follows an oath; μεθ' ὅρκων φάσκω is equivalent to ὄμνυμι. Ὄμνυμι, however, is often followed by μή in classical Greek: Demosthenes 21.119: ὤμνυε . . . μηδὲν εἰρηκέναι "He swore that he had said nothing."[73] The author of 2 Maccabees follows classical rules in his use of negatives with the infinitive.

(iii) Negatives with a Participle.

The basic rule in classical Greek for the negative used with participles is: οὐ when it states a fact, μή when it states a condition.[74]

"The post-classical language stongly tends towards μή with participles, whereas in classical Attic the decision to use μή depended on the meaning of the participle in each instance."[75] Within the NT, Turner shows that Luke-Acts uses οὐ with the participle more than other authors of the NT. 3 Maccabees uses both μή and οὐ with the participle: 3 Macc 3:11: οὐ καθορῶν τὸ τοῦ μεγίστου θεοῦ κράτος; 3 Macc 1:27: ἐπικαλεῖσθαι . . . μὴ παριδόντα τὴν ἄνομον . . . πρᾶξιν. For the usage of the papyri, Mayser has drawn up a table of comparison to show how μή intruded in the participial construction.[76] He shows that, in the 3rd cent. B.C.E., for forty correct uses of οὐ with the participle, there were nine cases where μή was used incorrectly with the participle. In the 2nd and 1st cent. B.C.E., the proportion had changed so that for every 27 correct uses of οὐ, there were 36 instances where μή was used incorrectly with the participle.

O. Birke has examined how Polybius negated the participle. While Polybius uses οὐ after verbs of perception, like ὁρῶ (whereas both Dionysius of Halicarnassus and Diodorus Siculus at times use μή, e.g., D.H. 6.40.3; D.S. 11.17.1), he does frequently use μή with circumstantial participles.[77] Plb 4.24.6: Λακεδαιμονίων δὲ μηδὲν εἰς τὴν κοινὴν συμμαχίαν ἐκφανὲς ἡμαρτηκότων "Since the Lacedemonians had committed no noticeable wrong against the common alliance." See also 18.7.5; 18.30.10. This use of μή with the circumstantial participle grows in Dionysius and Diodorus. At 11.65.4, Diodorus combines both constructions: καὶ τῶν Λακεδαιμονίων μὴ

---

[72] Εἶναι is presupposed from the first half of the indirect discourse: οὐκ (εἶναι) ὡς διαβάλλων ἦν ὁ δυσσεβὴς Σίμων.

[73] Smyth, *Greek Grammar*, 2725.

[74] Smyth, *Greek Grammar*, 2728.

[75] Moulton and Turner, *A Grammar*, 3.284.

[76] Mayser, *Grammatik*, 2.2/2.560-562.

[77] O. Birke, *De particularum*, 51-65.

δυναμένων βοηθῆσαι . . . ἄλλων δ' οὐκ ὄντων συμμάχων . . . "Since the Lacedemonians could not help . . . and there were no other allies . . ." Parthenius uses μή after a verb of perception at 15.3 (30,10): ἑώρων τὸν Λεύκιππον μὴ βουλόμενον "they saw that Leucippus was unwilling." With the circumstantial participle, Parthenius often uses μή incorrectly, e.g., 3.2 (9,4): τοῦ δὲ Ὀδυσσέως κατὰ τύχην τότε μὴ παρόντος "Ulysses happened to be from home." Within 2 Maccabees, the negative οὐ is used to negate participles at 2 Macc 4:5.6.34; 5:6.15.17; 6:26: 8:11; 9:18.22; 11:4; 14:6. At 6:4 (ἔτι δὲ τὰ μὴ καθήκοντα ἔνδον εἰσφερόντων "bringing into it forbidden things") and 6:9 (τοὺς δὲ μὴ προαιουμένους μεταβαίνειν ἐπὶ τὰ Ἑλληνικὰ κατασφάζειν "to slay anyone who would not adopt Greek customs"), μή is correctly used since the participle is generic. However, μή is used where οὐ should be at:

3:5 : καὶ νικῆσαι τὸν Ὀνίαν μὴ δυνάμενος ἦλθε
9:12: καὶ μηδὲ τῆς ὀσμῆς αὐτοῦ δυνάμενος ἀνέχεσθαι
10:13: μήτε εὐγενῆ τὴν ἐξουσίαν εὐγενίσας
11:24: ἀκηκοότες τοὺς Ἰουδαίους μὴ συνευδοκοῦντας τῇ . . . μεταθέσει
13:7 : συνέβη θανεῖν μηδὲ τῆς γῆς τυχόντα Μενέλαον

All these examples can be paralleled in Polybius, Diodorus Siculus, Dionysius of Halicarnassus, and Parthenius. With its proportion of 12 correct uses of οὐ with the participle to 5 incorrect uses of μή, the author of 2 Maccabees shows himself much more correct than the evidence from the papyri for the 2nd-1st cent B.C.E.

From an analysis of the negation, one can see that it is only with the participle that the intrusion of μή into the sphere of οὐ can be evidenced, an intrusion that is also found among other literary writers.

Hiatus:

The avoidance of hiatus, the break that occurs when a word ending with a vowel is immediately followed by a word beginning with a vowel, is a mark of literary style. Such avoidance, however, varies greatly from writer to writer. Dionysius of Halicarnassus distinguished three styles: the austere style allows hiatus freely (Thucydides); the middle style allows a little (Demosthenes); the smooth style avoids it carefully—Isocrates and Theopompus too carefully (*Comp* 22-23; *Dem* 4.38.40.43; *Isoc* 2; *Pomp* 6). Within 2nd-1st cent. B.C.E. writers, Polybius, Diodorus Siculus, and the stele of Antiochus of Commagene avoid hiatus carefully.[78]

---

[78] For Polybius, J. A. de Foucault, *Recherches*, 277-286; for Diodorus, J. Palm, *Über Sprache*, 28.204; for the Commagene stele, H. Dörrie, *Der Königskult des Antiochus von*

What of the author of 2 Maccabees? Richnow has addressed this question and has provided the basic data.[79] He has not compared the usage of 2 Maccabees, however, with other authors. In this section, the results of Richnow's work will be compared with those of M. D. Reeve on the Greek novelists, Heliodorus, Achilles Tatius, Chariton, and Longus.[80] Hiatus after καί and after the article is freely admitted by all the novelists and by the author of 2 Maccabees. The same is true for hiatus after sentences. 2 Maccabees also allows hiatus with μή and after verbs that end in -αι (i.e., when the accent is short, and thus always except in the aorist optative). This last was allowed in Attic comedy.[81] Demosthenes allowed hiatus after μή, as do the Greek novelists. Also included in such legitimate hiatus are those associated with monosyllables such as δέ, τε. Richnow also notes that hiatus is allowed in 2 Maccabees after some proper names (2 Macc 10:13; 12:30).

Richnow also holds that 2 Maccabees allows hiatus after the genitive singular ending -ου. Such hiatus was allowed by Galen.[82] There are 7 similar instances in Heliodorus, 6 in Achilles Tatius, perhaps 7 in Chariton, and 4 in Longus.[83] Two interesting cases of such hiatus are 2 Macc 2:22 and 4:25, for hiatus could have been easily avoided. 2:22: τοῦ κυρίου μετὰ πάσης ἐπιεικείας ἵλεως γενομένου αὐτοῖς. To avoid hiatus one would simply have had to place αὐτοῖς after ἵλεως. 4:25: θυμοὺς δὲ ὠμοῦ τυράννου καὶ θηρὸς βαρβάρου ὀργὰς ἔχων. By writing ὀργὰς βαρβάρου θηρὸς ἔχων, hiatus would have been avoided. In this last instance, Richnow states that hiatus was not avoided so that a chiasm could be formed:

θυμοὺς ὠμοῦ τυράννου
θηρὸς βαρβάρου ὀργὰς

Hiatus also occurs in 2 Maccabees at pausal points:
a) before a conditional sentence: 3:38 προσδέξῃ, ἐάνπερ
b) at cola: 9:4 αὐτῷ · οὕτως
   9:5 πληγῇ · ἄρτι
c) before a result clause: 12:9 σὺν τῷ στόλῳ, ὥστε
d) before an explanatory participle clause: 4:5 διεκομίσθη, οὐ γινόμενος

Kommagene im Lichte neuer Inschriften-Funde (Göttingen: Vandenhoeck & Ruprecht, 1964) 139: "Planmässig ist der Hiat vermieden."

[79] W. Richnow, "Untersuchungen," 108-115.

[80] M. D. Reeve, "Hiatus in the Greek Novelists," *Classical Quarterly* 21 (1971) 514-539.

[81] Reeve, "Hiatus," 515.

[82] Richnow refers to A. Minot, "De Galeni libris Περὶ δυσπνοίας" (Diss. Marburg, 1911) 50, Anm.1; J. Pertersen, "In Galeni de placitis Hippocratis et Platonis libros Quaestiones criticae" (Diss. Göttingen, 1888) 37-40.

[83] Reeve, "Hiatus," 520.524-525.527-528.

e) after a temporal phrase: 12:39 τῇ δὲ ἐχομένῃ ἦλθον
f) to mark off an adjectival phrase:
    8:9 παμφύλων ἔθνη οὐκ ἐλάττους τῶν δισμυρίων
    14:37 τῷ Νικάνορι ἀνὴρ φιλοπολίτης
g) to mark off a circumstantial participle phrase:
    3:33 τῷ Ἡλιοδώρῳ ἐν ταῖς αὐταῖς ἐσθήσεσιν ἐστολισμένοι
    4:50 ἔμενεν ἐπὶ τῇ ἀρχῇ ἐπιφυόμενος τῇ κακίᾳ
    5:11 τεθηριωμένος τῇ ψυχῇ ἔλαβε τὴν μὲν πόλιν
    5:21 ἐχωρίσθη οἰόμενος
    9:4 ἐπαρθεὶς δὲ τῷ θυμῷ ᾤετο
    9:21 περιπεσὼν ἀσθενείᾳ δυσχέρειαν ἐχούσῃ ἀναγκαῖον ἡγησάμην
    12:14 πεποιθότες . . . τῇ τε τῶν βρωμάτων παραθέσει ἀναγωγότερον
    12:16 καταλαβόμενοί τε τὴν πόλιν τῇ τοῦ θεοῦ θελήσει ἀμυθήτους ·
    12:38 ἀναλαβὼν τὸ στράτευμα ἧκεν εἰς Οδολλαμ πόλιν
    15:21 συνιδὼν . . . τήν τε τῶν θηρίων ἀγριότητα ἀνατείνας τὰς χεῖρας

M. D. Reeve has several examples where hiatus is used in each of the Greek novelists to mark such phrases.

Hiatus occurs 4 times before οὖν (2 Macc 6:12; 9:11; 11:25.26), as in Chariton, with 24 in Achilles Tatius.[84] Twice it occurs before the augmented verb (2 Macc 4:32 ἕτερα ἐτύγχανε; 11:5 τοῦτο ἔθλιβεν), a type of hiatus which is found 5 times in Heliodorus, 8 in Achilles Tatius, and 5 times in Chariton.

13 examples of hiatus remain in 2 Maccabees:
    3:37 ποῖός τις εἴη ἐπιτήδειος
    3:38 Εἴ τινα ἔχεις πολέμιον
    6:29 ὡς αὐτοὶ ὑπελάμβανον, but q 1-542 58 771 read διελάμβανον
    7:24 ἐπίστου ἅμα, but V reads ἅμα in a different location
    7:36 ἡμέτεροι ἀδελφοί
    10:13 ἐμπιστευθέντα ὑπό
    10:35 προσβαλόντες τῷ τείχει ἀρρενωδῶς
    11:8 ἐν λευκῇ ἐσθῆτι
    11:19 τὴν εἰς τὰ πράγματα εὔνοιαν
    13:26 ἀπελογήσατο ἐνδεχομένως
    14:16 συμμίσγει αὐτοῖς, but L' La^LXVP Sy read συμμίσγουσιν
    14:29 τῷ βασιλεῖ ἀντιπράττειν
    15:2 τῇ προτετιμημένῃ ὑπὸ τοῦ πάντα ἐφορῶντος . . . ἡμέρᾳ

M. D. Reeve has found 20 such singularities in Heliodorus, 42 in Achilles Tatius, and 40 in Chariton.[85] In more than one instance, he suggests slight

---

84 Reeve, "Hiatus," 521.527.
85 Reeve, "Hiatus," 520-521.524-525.527-528.

emendation to avoid hiatus. The only edition which includes the novelists and 2 Maccabees which I could find for the sake of page comparison was that of *Scriptorum Graecorum Bibliotheca* (Paris: F. Didot, 1885) vols. 18 and 61. Using this edition for statistical purposes, one finds 1 singularity per 9.35 pages for Heliodorus, 1 per 2.4 pages for Achilles Tatius, 1 per 2.2 pages for Chariton, and 1 per 2.6 pages for 2 Maccabees.

From this comparison of the avoidance of hiatus in 2 Maccabees and in the Greek novelists, one can see that the author of 2 Maccabees was as careful as Achilles Tatius and Chariton were in his attempt to write a good, literary style. Such a conclusion reinforces the results of the examination of the syntax of 2 Maccabees.

Rhetorical Figures:

The author of 2 Maccabees loves words, he delights in tossing them around and playing them off one another, in straining their meaning to the limit. As Gil and Richnow have richly documented, the author of 2 Maccabees employs alliteration (cf. 12:14: πεποιθότες τῇ τῶν τειχέων ἐρυμνότητι τῇ τε τῶν βρωμάτων παραθέσει), the use of homoioteleuta (cf. 14:45: φερομένων κρουνηδὸν τῶν αἱμάτων καὶ δυσχερῶν τῶν τραυμάτων ὄντων) and metaphors—"burning with anger" (4:38; 10:35; 14:45), and all the "beast" metaphors: "flying like lions against the enemy" (11:11), "beastly in spirit" (5:11). But the images are stereotype. What is new are the words: λεοντηδόν (11:11), κρουνηδόν (14:45), ἀγεληδόν (3:18; 14:14). The author of 2 Maccabees has employed unusual or infrequent words normally found among the poets,[86] and hapax legomena abound. Most of the rhetorical effect in 2 Maccabees comes from word-play. At the lowest rung is litotes, affirmation expressed by the negative of the contrary as, e.g., οὐκ ὀλίγους (8:6; 10:24; 14:30),[87] and groupings of two or three phrases: 6:31:τὸν ἑαυτοῦ θάνατον ὑπόδειγμα γενναιότητος καὶ μνημόσυνον ἀρετῆς; 3:26: τῇ ῥώμῃ μὲν ἐκπρεπεῖς, κάλλιστοι δὲ τὴν δόξαν, διαπρεπεῖς δὲ τὴν περιβολήν; 4:42: πολλοὺς μὲν αὐτῶν τραυματίας ἐποίησαν, τινὰς δὲ καὶ κατέβαλον, πάντας δὲ εἰς φυγὴν συνήλασαν; 5:13: νέων καὶ πρεσβυτέρων ἀναιρέσεις, γυναικῶν καὶ τέκνων ἀφανισμός, παρθένων τε καὶ νηπίων σφαγαί. Besides these,

---

[86] Poetic words like ἄτερ (12:15), ῥωμάλεοι (12:27), ἀεννάου (7:36), οἰωνοβρώτοος (9:15), as well as neologisms like συμμισοπονηρεῖν (4:36), ὑπονοθεύειν (4:7), δυσπέτημα (5:20), θαυμασμοῦ (7:19), etc. One should note here the use of the preposition ὡς at 2 Macc 4:5 (πρός in A′ L 311). This preposition is not found in Aristotle, the LXX, the NT, or the papyri. For a full discussion and listing of these unusual words, see Richnow, "Untersuchung," 48-58.

[87] There are 10 examples in 2 Maccabees, none in 1 Maccabees. For its use in Polybius and Diodorus Siculus, see J. Palm, *Über Sprache*, 155-156.

there is parallelism and antithesis: 2:32: τὸ μὲν πρὸ τῆς ἱστορίας πλεονάζειν, τὴν δὲ ἱστορίαν ἐπιτέμνειν; 3:30: τὸ μικρῷ πρότερον δέους καὶ ταραχῆς γέμον ἱερὸν . . . χαρᾶς καὶ εὐφροσύνης ἐπεπλήρωτο; 6:19: τὸν μετ' εὐκλείας θάνατον μᾶλλον ἤ τὸν μετὰ μύσους βίον. Again there is chiastic structure: 4:25: θυμοὺς δὲ ὠμοῦ τυράννου καὶ θηρὸς βαρβάρου ὀργὰς ἔχων; 9:24: ἐάν τι παράδοξον ἀποβαίνῃ ἤ καὶ προσαγγελῇ τι δυσχερές; 5:19: οὐ διὰ τὸν τόπον τὸ ἔθνος, ἀλλὰ διὰ τὸ ἔθνος τὸν τόπον (chiasm not from the point of view of syntax, but of words used); 4:26: ὁ τὸν ἴδιον ἀδελφὸν ὑπονοθεύσας ὑπονοθευθεὶς ὑφ' ἑτέρου. With this last example, one comes to a whole range of word-plays: 5:6: τὴν εἰς τοὺς συγγενεῖς εὐημερίαν δυσημερίαν εἶναι τὴν μεγίστην; 5:20: συμμετασχὼν τῶν τοῦ ἔθνους δυσπετημάτων γενομένων ὕστερον εὐεργετημάτων; 6:29: τὴν μικρῷ πρότερον εὐμένειαν εἰς δυσμένειαν; 14:6: στασιάζουσιν οὐκ ἐῶντες τὴν βασιλείαν εὐσταθείας τυχεῖν; 15:36: μηδαμῶς ἐᾶσαι ἀπαράσημαντον τήνδε τὴν ἡμέραν, ἔχειν δὲ ἐπίσημον. There are also numerous repetitions of the same words or stems: 3:15 τὸν περὶ παρακαταθήκης νομοθετήσαντα τοῖς παρακατατεθεμένοις; 3:22: τὰ πεπιστευμένα τοῖς πεπιστευκόσι σῷα διαφυλάσσειν; 10:26: ἐχθρεῦσαι τοῖς ἐχθροῖς αὐτῶν καὶ ἀντικεῖσθαι τοῖς ἀντικειμένοις; 12:42: τὸ γεγενὸς ἁμάρτημα . . . αὐτοὺς ἀναμαρτήτους . . . διὰ τὴν ἁμαρτίαν. Finally, one should mention the variations in words used to express the same idea as at 5:16 (ταῖς μιεραῖς χερσὶ . . . ταῖς βεβήλοις χερσί), but especially the number of words used for "to die": χειρώσασθαι (4:34.42); παρέκλεισεν (4:34); ἀπεκόσμησε (4:38); προπέμπειν εἰς τὸν ᾅδην (6:23); προσωθοῦσιν εἰς ὄλεθρον (13:6). In this connection should be marked the various epithets used for God:

3:36: τοῦ μεγίστου θεοῦ; 3:39: ὁ τὴν κατοικίαν ἐπουράνιον ἔχων; 3:22: τὸν παγκράτη κύριον; 3:24: ὁ τῶν πνευμάτων καὶ πάσης ἐξουσίας δυνάστης; 3:31: τὸν ὕψιστον; 5:17: ὁ δεσπότης; 7:23: ὁ τοῦ κόσμου κτίστης, ὁ πλάσας ἀνθρώπου γένεσιν καὶ πάντων ἐξευρὼν γένεσιν; 7:33: ὁ ζῶν κύριος; 7:35: τοῦ παντοκράτορος ἐπόπτου θεοῦ; 9:5: παντεπόπτης κύριος; 12:6: τὸν δίκαιον κριτὴν θεόν; 11:13: τοῦ δυναμένου θεοῦ; 12:15: τὸν μέγαν τοῦ κόσμου δυνάστην; 12:22 τοῦ τὰ πάντα ἐφορῶντος; 12:28: τὸν δυνάστην τὸν μετὰ κράτους συντρίβοντα τὰς τῶν πολεμίων ὁλκάς; 12:41: τοῦ δικαιοκρίτου κυρίου τοῦ τὰ κεκρυμμένα φανερὰ ποιοῦντος; 13:4: ὁ δὲ βασιλεὺς τῶν βασιλέων; 13:14: τῷ κτίστῃ τοῦ κόσμου; 14:15: τὸν ἄχρι αἰῶνος συστήσαντα τὸν ἑαυτοῦ λαόν, ἀεὶ δὲ μετ' ἐπιφανείας ἀντιλαμβανόμενον τῆς ἑαυτοῦ μερίδος; 14:36: ἅγιε παντὸς ἁγιασμοῦ κύριε; 14:34: τὸν διὰ παντὸς ὑπέρμαχον τοῦ ἔθνους ἡμῶν; 14:46: τὸν δεσπόζοντα τῆς ζωῆς καὶ τοῦ πνεύματος; 15:21: τὸν τερατοποιὸν κύριον; 15:23: δυνάστα τῶν οὐρανῶν; 15:29: τὸν δυνάστην.

This emphasis on words and phrases as the main carriers of his rhetorical coloring is also reflected in the word order of 2 Maccabees. The phrases are grouped together, and there are no major separations of syntactically grouped units. When there is separation, it is usually only by one word being inserted: 6:4: ὑπὸ τῶν ἐθνῶν ἐπεπλήρωτο ῥᾳθυμούντων; 6:20: καθ᾽ ὅν ἔδει τρόπον; 7:14: τὰς ὑπὸ τοῦ θεοῦ προσδοκᾶν ἐλπίδας. Such separation can be compared with the type generally found in Diodorus Siculus and described as mild:[88] 1.58.1-2: συμπτώματι δὲ περιέπεσεν ἰδιάζοντι, οὐδεμιᾶς ἐτύγχανε πολυωρίας. Palm contrasts this type of separation with that of Dionysius of Halicarnassus (3.32.3: πεῖραν ἐβούλοντο ἑτέρου λαβεῖν ἀγῶνος) and the Letter of Aristeas (78: ὅτε πρὸς τὴν τῶν ἀργορῶν προσβλέψαι τις θέσιν ἤθελεν). There is certainly separation of article and its substantive in 2 Maccabees, the most notable example being 15:18: ἦν γὰρ ὁ περὶ γυναικῶν καὶ τέκνων, ἔτι δὲ ἀδελφῶν καὶ συγγενῶν ἐν ἥττονι μέρει κείμενος αὐτοῖς, μέγιστος δὲ καὶ πρῶτος ὁ περὶ τοῦ καθηγιασμένου ναοῦ φόβος. Palm has shown how this separation reflects a desire to unite all those elements which belong together, and that it is found throughout the literature of the Hellenistic period, but not frequently in the papyri. He concludes that this stylistic feature results from the increasing use of substantives. Those who use this technique are mainly concerned to gather together, within the article and the substantive, all the factors qualifying that substantive.[89]

This attempt at gathering all related material together is also seen in certain asyndeta. 14:25: παρεκάλεσεν αὐτὸν γῆμαι καὶ παιδοποιήσασθαι, ἐγάμησεν, εὐστάθησεν, ἐκοινώνησε βίου; 13:19: προσῆγεν, ἐτροποῦτο, προσέκρουεν, ἠλαττονοῦτο; also 13:21-26. Here the asyndeta provide a rapid overview of what happened.[90] At 13:14 also, the asyndetic grouping of περὶ νόμων, ἱεροῦ, πόλεως, πατρίδος, πολιτείας shows the close connection which binds these together, and provides a quick rundown of Judas' speech.

Rhetorical figures do not belong to any one period, but the emphasis in 2 Maccabees on unusual words, on using words or phrases as contrasts to or complements of other words or phrases,[91] and on the grouping of the ele-

---

[88] J. Palm, Über Sprache, 131-135.

[89] J. Palm, Über Sprache, 137.

[90] Kühner-Gerth (Ausführliche Grammatik 2.340) provide an example from Xenophon HG 4.3.19: συμβαλόντες τὰς ἀσπίδας ἐωθοῦντο, ἐμάχοντο, ἀπέκτεινον, ἀπέθησκον "setting shields against shields they shoved, fought, killed, and were killed."

[91] Awareness of this tendency of the author may help in certain passages. For example, 4:14: ὥστε μηκέτι περὶ τὰς τοῦ θυσιαστηρίου λειτουργίας προθύμους εἶναι τοὺς ἱερεῖς, ἀλλὰ . . . ἔσπευδον μετέχειν τῆς ἐν παλαίστρῃ παρανόμου χορηγίας. Here it is almost impossible to translate χορηγίας. Abel suggested that "La palestre qui est une des parties du gymnase réservée à la lutte, sert à designer parfois le gymnase dans sa totalité. Le mot de chorégie peut avoir également une extension analogue. Il ne s'agit plus ici de l'entretien d'un choeur au théâtre, ni

ments of the sentence into units, reflects the same importance of substantives as found in Polybius and Diodorus Siculus.[92]

Conclusion:

As stated in the introduction to this chapter, the concern was to isolate certain syntactic elements in the narrative of 2 Maccabees which would bear comparison with other Hellenistic writings as well as to point out certain rhetorical features of the style of 2 Maccabees. The syntactic analysis was necessarily limited and the object was not to show how, in many ways, 2 Maccabees is a typical product of the Hellenistic age—e.g., in the increased use of the articular infinitive,[93] in the greater use of abstract substantives with prepositions.[94] Such is to be expected.

même d'un concours gymnique organisé aux frais d'un gymnasiarque, mais de l'entraînement journalier auquel se livraient en public les habitués du sport." (Abel, *Les Livres*, 334.) Au contraire, the author is playing on words again: he is contrasting χορηγία with λειτουργία—a fine opposition, as χορηγία was often used to mean "public services." See, e.g., the conjunction in Demosthenes' *Against Leptines* 19: "Let us then see what additional contributors (χορηγούς) he provides to perform those public services (εἰς ἐκείνας τὰς λητουργίας). Now the richest citizens, when equipping a war-galley, are already exempt from the ordinary services (τῶν χορηγιῶν ἀτελαῖς). . . ." One should nuance the translation of 2 Macc 4:14 to contrast the illegal ministry in the palestra with the ministry round the altar.

[92] One should perhaps comment here on the thesis of Gil ("Sobre el estilo") and Richnow ("Untersuchungen") that 2 Maccabees belongs to the style of Asianism. Unfortunately, both Gil and Richnow defined Asianic style according to the statements of E. Norden (*Die antike Kunstprosa* [Leipzig/Berlin: Teubner, 1st ed. 1898, 2nd ed. 1915] 1.131-149), without noticing the qualifications made necessary by the article of U. von Moellendorff-Wilamowitz ("Asianismus und Atticismus," *Hermes* 35 [1900] 1-52). Asianism is not a positive term denoting a certain style of writing, but a purely negative condemnation of the way certain writers from Asia Minor spoke and wrote Greek. Asianism was not a literary movement, and should not be identified with Hellenistic literature in general, as the study of C. Wooten ("Le développement du style asiastique pendant l'époque hellénistique," *Revue des Études Grecques* 88 [1975] 94-104) has shown. As part of their attempt to link 2 Maccabees with Asianism, both Gil and Richnow have pointed to prose-rhythm elements in 2 Maccabees. While isolated passages may evidence heightened prose-rhythm, my own study of 2 Maccabees 3 and 4 revealed no consistently applied rhythmic or prosodic system at the end of cola, as has been found in the stele of Commagene. There is no reason to apply the label "Asianic" to 2 Maccabees.

[93] One should note here, for example, the tendency of the author of 2 Maccabees to use the articular infinitive with prepositions: εἰς (2:25, 6:27); διά (3:38; 4:18.30; 6.11.24.29; 8:36; 10:13; 15:17); πρός (4:46; 5:27; 6:20; 7:14); and once each with περί (3:6), ὑπέρ (4:36), μεχρί (6:14), and ἐκ (7:9).

[94] Note, for example, the superfluous use of the preposition where the simple genitive would have been sufficient: 3:14 τὴν περὶ τούτων ἐπίσκεψιν; 6:21: τῶν ἀπὸ τῆς θυσίας κρεῶν; 10:21: τοὺς πολεμίους κατ' αὐτῶν. There is also the wide use in 2 Maccabees of the verb + abstract in place of the simple verb, e.g., 3:8: ἐποιεῖτο τὴν πορείαν.

What I did find was that in various ways, from matters of accidence and orthography to the use of the future tense, 2 Maccabees consistently showed a nicety of syntax that one associates with classical, literary writers. The author shows himself capable of writing good Greek, he is particular in his word choice. In sum, one has in 2 Maccabees the work of someone trained in the schools of rhetoric.

CHAPTER THREE

THE STRUCTURE OF THE NARRATIVE*

In the previous chapter, the author of the epitome was seen to have at his command a wide range of vocabulary, a good grasp of syntax, and an attention to stylistic demands. In this present chapter, I shall examine how the author has proceeded on another level of literary production, on the level of the structure of the contents of the narrative.

2 Macc 3:1-40: The Repulse of Heliodorus:

The first major event in the narrative of 2 Maccabees is the attack of Heliodorus on the temple in Jerusalem and his repulse. The attack is placed in the time of Seleucus IV Philopator, who ruled from 187 to 175 B.C.E. Before the attack, Jerusalem had been in peace, the laws were observed, and the temple was honored even by foreign kings (2 Macc 3:1). The frame for the attack is provided by the intrigues of a certain temple official, Simon,[1] to unseat the holy high-priest Onias. Simon's first attempt leads him to inform against Onias to the Seleucid bureaucracy. Heliodorus' mission is the result of this information. The spectacular failure of this venture does not daunt Simon—in 2 Macc 4:1-3, he blames Onias for the attack on Heliodorus, and so the narrative moves on.

The story as it stands has all the earmarks of accounts written in praise of a deity who defends his/her temple or city. I hesitate to call these battle accounts examples of the same literary form, because the ways in which the deities defend their temples are so various that no tight, recurring order of content emerges. A general shared pattern is found, grounded no doubt in the way real life battles occur: the attackers approach, the defenders ask help of the deity, the deity responds, the attackers are repulsed, and the defenders rejoice. I call this pattern a topos, a term which has looser connotations than form but which is not so controversial as motif or theme.

---

* A condensed version of some sections of this chapter first appeared in "2 Maccabees and 'Tragic History'" *HUCA* 50 (1979) 107-114, and there is some overlap in word choice.

[1] With Hanhart, Habicht, and Tcherikover (for a full discussion, see Tcherikover, *Hellenistic Civilisation*, 403-404), I read βαλγεα.

That it was customary for cities to celebrate the epiphanies of their patron deity can be gauged from the inscriptions honoring such epiphanies. One of the well-known examples is the inscription from Cos in which an invitation is extended to celebrate the repulse of the Gauls from Delphi by Apollo in 279 B.C.E. This epiphany of Apollo was elaborated in the account by Pausanias.[2] From Panamaros comes an inscription detailing how Zeus Panamaros defended the city,[3] and the Lindos Chronicle, a more literary effort where historians are given as sources for the account, tells how the citizens were delivered from a siege of the Persians by the miraculous intervention of Athene.[4] A local historian, Syriscus, was honored by the citizens of Chersonesus for his history of the city, which placed particular emphasis on the divine help extended to the city by Athene.[5] Herodotus recounts the defense of Delphi by Apollo against marauding Persians.[6] Such accounts are, however, not confined to Greek tradition. One finds a similar defense of a temple in the account of Kuturnaḫḫunte in the Kedorlaomer inscription.[7] Within the biblical tradition, the repulse of Sennacherib when he attacked Jerusalem and King Hezekiah is similar (2 Chr 32:1-22; 2 Kgs 18:17-19:36). In this narrative, Hezekiah exhorts the people to be strong and not afraid "for there is one greater with us than with him," while the commanders of Sennacherib state that the God of Israel will be no more effective against Assyrian might than the gods of other nations had been. At this, Hezekiah and the prophet Isaiah pray to God. The Lord sends an angel to destroy the Assyrians. Sennacherib is forced to retreat in shame, while the Jews have peace restored.[8]

The story of Heliodorus, then, should be ranged alongside such accounts where the topos, a deity defending his/her city or temple, is found. The account in 2 Maccabees is highly stylized. One factor which helps toward such a dramatization lies in the nature of the confrontation. In 2 Maccabees, it is a legal controversy over the ownership of the money in the

[2]   Paus 10.23.2; Justin 24.8.3; D.S. 22.9. For a full discussion, see G. Nachtergael, *Les Galates en Grèce et les Sôtéria de Delphes. Recherches d'histoire et d'épigraphie hellénistiques.* Mémoires de l'Académie royale de Belgique 63. Brussels: Palais des Académies, 1977.
[3]   P. Roussel, "Le miracle de Zeus Panamaros," *Bulletin de Correspondance Hellénique* 55 (1931) 70-116.
[4]   FGH 532.
[5]   FGH 807 T 1. Cf. M. Rostowzew, "Ἐπιφάνειαι," *Klio* 16 (1919-20) 203-206.
[6]   Hdt 8. 35-39.
[7]   N. Stokholm, "Zür Überlieferung von Heliodor (2 Makk.3), Kuturnaḫḫunte, und anderen missglückten Tempelräubern," *ST* 22 (1968) 1-28.
[8]   Cf. the repulse of the Assyrians invading Egypt by divinely sent field mice in Hdt 2.141.

temple, i.e., whether they are unused kingly funds or not.[9] In the other extant accounts of attacks on temples, normally a huge force is sent to the attack or plunder. The fact that it is a legal controversy in 2 Maccabees allows the author to focus on the one-on-one confrontation between Heliodorus and Onias. The protection of the city will not be by a general rout of the besiegers, but by the sudden reversal of fortune of the all-powerful Seleucid minister who, though surrounded by his bodyguards, cannot escape punishment. Such is the stuff of drama, and the author exploits it to the hilt, both in his use of contrast and antithesis in the actual epiphany (3:28-30), as well as in his preparation for the event where he paints the tearful sorrow of the inhabitants. 2 Macc 3:15-22 are full of rhetorical embellishments: the unusual words (*deos ti kai phrikasmos*; *ageledon*); the repetition of the same root to create word-play (*ton peri parakatathekes nomothetesanta tois parakatathemenois*; *ta pepisteumena tois pepisteukosi*); the heightened clustering of phrases (*hai men synetrechon epi tous pylonas, hai de epi ta teiche, tines de dia ton thyridon diekypton, pasai de . . .*). All this description of great emotion only serves to underline the great reversal that follows, with its corresponding joy for the city.[10] The temple has to be protected.

Since there is such a one-on-one confrontation at the heart of the narrative, certain problems arise. When Heliodorus is struck down by the onrushing attack of the deity's angels, is he to stay down? In the Kedorlaomer texts, the leader of the attackers is bound in some mysterious way, and nothing more is heard of him. In Herodotus' account of the attack on Delphi by the Persians, some of the attacking force survive, some do not. When Sennacherib's siege of Jerusalem is divinely broken, many of his forces perish, but Sennacherib himself survives. When only one person is involved in the confrontation, how can the divine fury attack that person directly, and yet not destroy him? Heliodorus, however, could not die in Jerusalem, for he has to appear again on the stage of history to kill Seleucus IV by treachery.

A somewhat similar problem faced the author of the account that lies behind the Lindos Chronicle epiphany. Datis, the Persian commander, and his forces were not destroyed at Lindos, but took part in the battle at Marathon. How can they undergo an attack by a deity and yet sail away

---

[9]   E. Bickermann, "Héliodore au temple de Jérusalem," 6-18. Tcherikover (*Hellenistic Civilisation*, 465-466) has shown that Bickermann's attempt to translate διάφορα (3:6) as surplus resources overloads the word, which can simply mean "money." However, Bickermann is right in that the dispute arises from the confusion of public money and private deposits.

[10] E. Bickermann ("Héliodore au temple de Jérusalem," 21-22) states without proof that 2 Macc 3:14-22 are from the hand of a redactor who links the two versions of the Heliodorus story (see chap. one, 19-21). Bickermann states that, at v 23, one comes back to the same position as at v 13. However, he overlooks the fact that that is precisely why an inchoate imperfect is used at both v 14 and v 23: *eisēei; epetelei*.

unharmed? The problem is solved in the Lindos account by having the Persian host suffer a miraculous thirst, while the drought of the besieged is broken by a geographically limited rainfall. This miracle of nature is not destructive of the Persian host, and their leader survives to proclaim the greatness of the goddess Athene. This witness by the defeated Persian to the power of the Greek goddess was one of many propaganda stories emanating from regions which had not been part of the league to withstand the Persians, but which were anxious, after the fact, to range themselves alongside the victorious Greeks.[11]

2 Maccabees, however, does not employ a nature miracle but a full-scale appearance of two young men whipping Heliodorus.[12] With such divine punishment, how can Heliodorus survive? The author has recourse to a miraculous cure of Heliodorus, in which the same two young men take part. The emphasis in the account, however, is not on the miraculous healing, for this is mentioned almost incidentally: *dia gar auton soi kecharistai to zēn ho kyrios.* Rather, what is underlined is the propaganda aspect: the two young men commission Heliodorus to proclaim the greatness of Israel's God. 2 Maccabees 3 has this propaganda aspect in common with the account of the Lindos Chronicle, where the enemy himself is forced to proclaim the greatness of the deity. In 2 Maccabees, there are other instances of such witness: at 2 Macc 8:36, Nicanor proclaims the sovereignty of the God of Israel, and Antiochus IV promises to do so at 2 Macc 9:17. When the Jews conquer Nicanor in the final battle in 2 Maccabees, they proclaim God's greatness, much as the Panamarians do at the repulse of their attackers: "Great is Zeus Panamaros."[13] Such propaganda may also lie behind the story in Herodotus: "There is a story, I am told, amongst those who got away, that there was yet another miraculous occurrence: they saw, so they said, two gigantic soldiers— taller than ever a man was—pursuing them and cutting them down."[14] Such a story in the mouth of the defeated Persians betrays the same propaganda

---

[11] P. Faure, "La conduite des armées perses à Rhodes pendant la première guerre médique," *Revue historique* 192 (1941) 236-241. Faure writes: "C'est à croire que le récit lindien—habile dans son genre, quant à la variété, la foi patriotique et la piété—aurait été composé de tous les fragments épars de l'histoire édifiante contemporaine. Après la victoire grecque, il fut bon de se vanter d'une fidélité à la cause alliée—ou d'une intrépidité—qu'on n'avait pas toujours eues" (239-240).

[12] See chap. one, 18-19; 19-21.

[13] Panamaros inscription, 1.13.

[14] Hdt 8.38. Here one could mention the comment of P. Roussel on the Zeus Panamaros inscription: "Notre document, qui se place peu après le milieu du Ier siècle av.J.-C., n'est pas un simple hommage au dieu; comme toute la littérature arétalogique, il tend, en augmentant sa gloire, à grossir le nombre des fidèles qui, aux jours des grands pèlerinages vers le haut lieu, répéteront avec les témoins du miracle officiellement authentiqué par un decret: Μέγας ὁ Ζεὺς Πανάμαρος." (P. Roussel, "Le miracle," 116.)

tendency. Who would be concerned to circulate such stories except devotees of the deity in question?

The answer in 2 Maccabees 3 to the problem of the reappearance of the divinely punished attacker differs in significant detail from the ways in which 3 and 4 Maccabees answer the same problem. In 3 Macc 2:21-24, the insolent Ptolemy does not die in Jerusalem, yet he is repulsed from the temple by divine interference. Since the narrative of 3 Maccabees centers around the persecution of the Jews by the same Ptolemy, at this opening juncture of the story it would be too early for Ptolemy to proclaim the superiority of Israel's God and would detract from the climax when he finally does so (3 Macc 6:22-7:9). The author of 3 Maccabees simply has Ptolemy revive after a few days and return to Egypt to carry out his wicked designs against the Jews. The model here might be the behavior of the Pharaoh in the Exodus narrative, who hardens his heart again after each plague and does not repent. In 4 Macc 4:1-14, the problem involved in combining such a dramatic confrontation between the attacker and the deity with a proclamation by the defeated attacker of the sovereignty of the deity has been eliminated. The author has the attacker fall, but only half-dead. The defeated attacker can thus beseech healing and forgiveness on his own behalf. The need for friends to do so, as in 2 Macc 3:31, is avoided, and there is no awkward transition from the prostrate attacker to his miraculous revival. Again, in 4 Macc 4:12, the attacker promises of his own accord to hymn the greatness of Israel's God—he is not commissioned to do so by another appearance. The whole presentation in 4 Macc 4:1-14 is thus more streamlined and has the advantage of no shift in scene. However, by such streamlining the divine commission is lost, and no mention is made of the actual proclamation by the defeated attacker. In contrast to 2 Maccabees, this witness is not an interest of the author of 4 Maccabees.

The controversy over the repayment of money to Seleucus IV and the successful non-payment by the Jews is the second of three attempts by Simon to embarrass Onias and rob him of authority. As such, it provides another example of the tensions and factions within Jerusalem at that time, but it hardly deserves the elaborate treatment it receives in 2 Maccabees. It is, after all, an isolated incident which does not influence further historical developments: the epiphany does not stop Simon from continuing his scheming; it does not cause any further action from Seleucus to gain the money or to renounce completely claims to it—the dialogue at 2 Macc 3:37-39 is a comic foil to re-emphasize the events of the epiphany and once again proclaim the sovereignty of the God of Israel. This historically minor event, however, gains importance from a literary point of view. The author has well fitted the story into the overall narrative. The reason why Onias prays for the healing of Heliodorus at 3:32 prepares the way for the further

development of the story where Simon uses the same argument to accuse
Onias of machinations against Heliodorus (4:1-2). 2 Maccabees 3 is thus part
of the build-up of the work in its literary process. Its importance lies beyond
this. In the prologue to the narrative, the author had promised epiphanies
whereby the God of Israel defended his land (2:21-22). 2 Maccabees 3, the
first section of the book, is devoted to such an epiphany. The narrative is
strongly biased towards propaganda to proclaim the greatness of the God of
Israel, who protects the temple at Jerusalem.[15] 2 Maccabees 3 shows already
that one is dealing with a devotee of the God of Israel.

2 Macc 4:1-10:9: The Profanation of the Temple and its Renewal:

The next major section of the narrative deals with the profanation of the
temple and the persecution of the people as well as the restoration of the
temple and the punishment of the attacker, Antiochus IV. I shall first deal
with the outbreak of evil, and then with the restoration.

A. 2 Macc 4:1-7:42: The Assault of Evil.

This section of the narrative is unified through the description of the
assault of evil on the Jews, which reaches its climax in the persecutions. First
within the complex comes the increasing violence of Simon against Onias,
who departs for Antioch. Onias is replaced in the high-priesthood by his
brother Jason, who buys the office. This in itself is an initial step towards the
Hellenization of the Jewish people. Jason pushes forward with his innova-
tions. The desire to imitate the customs of the Greeks is shown in the partici-
pation in the games at Tyre and in the way in which Antiochus IV is received
in Jerusalem. Jason is portrayed as wanting to follow Greek customs even to
the extent of dedicating an offering to Hercules, and Antiochus IV is
received in Jerusalem with all the trappings of a Hellenistic king.[16] Jason in
his turn is supplanted by Menelaus, the brother of that Simon who had been
so antagonistic towards the pious Onias. Menelaus' rule is characterized by
intrigues, which result in the murder of the former high-priest Onias (2 Macc

---

[15] One should notice that an epiphany guaranteed the right of asylum to Magnesia, and
that this was commemorated by yearly games in honor of Artemis. Cf. O. Kern, *Die Inschriften
von Magnesia am Maeander* (Berlin: W. Spemann, 1900), nos. 16-73.

[16] For the ceremonial character of the reception of a king in the city of his realm, see
C. Habicht, *Gottmenschentum und griechische Städte* (Zetemata: Monographien zur klassischen Altertumswissenschaft, 14; 2nd ed.; Munich: Beck, 1970) 234. One should note that the
use of the word *dadouchia*, a word usually reserved for the Eleusinian mysteries, appears to
indicate further Hellenization on Jason's part.

4:27-33), and in the execution of ambassadors sent to complain of the pillaging tactics of Menelaus and his lieutenant Lysimachus.

After their customs had been changed and their temple robbed, the Jews still had worse to come: the military intervention of Antiochus IV and the regulations imposed against the practice of their Law. That Antiochus should interfere because of the rivalry between Jason and Menelaus is what can be expected once Jerusalem had become a city like all others. The regulations imposed by Antiochus are the final step in the attempt to assimilate the Jews to other nations.

This process, however, is not to be accomplished easily. First comes the tale of the deaths of two women who circumcised their children (2 Macc 6:10), then the deaths of those trying to celebrate the Sabbath in secret (2 Macc 6:11). These first persecutions are only the lead-up to the detailed accounts of the deaths of Eleazar (2 Macc 6:18-31), and of a mother and her seven sons (2 Macc 7:1-41).

The events narrated in 2 Macc 4:1-7:42 cover a time span of over eight years,[17] and yet are linked together as they show how evil came upon the Jewish people. The attempt to change the laws of the people by Jason led to the tyrannous behavior of Menelaus and Antiochus IV. This topical collection of the events of those years is in fact underscored by two major digressions or reflections of the epitomizer. The first (2 Macc 5:17-20) explained how God's temple could be pillaged by Antiochus IV, and why it was not defended by God as at the attempt of Heliodorus. The explanation lies in the sins of the people—once God's anger over their sins is appeased, the temple will be restored. The second reflection (2 Macc 6:12-17) is a preface to the martyrdoms. It explains the horrors of the persecutions by appeal to a principle similar to "Spare the rod, spoil the child."[18] Both digressions deal with the theological problem of how Israel, as God's chosen people, could

---

[17] From the death of Seleucus IV Eupator in the sixth month of 137th year sel.bab., i.e., 3-22 Sept., 175, to some time after the profanation of the temple in December 167 (acc. to 1 Macc 1:54-59). See Bunge, *Untersuchungen*, 622-625.

[18] The theology here is opposite in many ways to that of the Wisdom of Solomon (11:10-12:27) and Sirach (5:4-9; 18:10-14). In those books, it is a question of God's forbearance towards other nations so that they might have time to repent, as in Romans 2:4. This is not the case in 2 Macc 6:12-17, where the premise is that all men sin, but that God has Israel suffer and pay for its sins now, so that it will not have to pay for their cumulative effect later. By so punishing them, God is not allowing Israel to fall into sinful habits, which is why I used the analogy of "Spare the rod, spoil the child." This "Pay now, play later" approach is in line with the Rabbinic teaching on the goodness of suffering in that it leads to the future world. See G. Foot Moore, *Judaism in the First Centuries of the Christian Era* (Cambridge: Harvard Univ. Press, 1966) 2.248-256. As regards the use of "benefactor" language in this digression, see S. Mott, "The Greek Benefactor and Deliverance from Moral Distress" (unpublished PhD dissertation, Harvard University, 1971).

undergo such persecutions, and both point ahead to times of mercy. In this function, they carry on the role already played by the reflection at 2 Macc 4:16-17. Immediately after Jason had taken his first steps to Hellenize the Jews, the author states: "As a result a difficult situation encompassed them, and those whose mode of life they were striving after and whom they were wishing to imitate exactly became their enemies and punished them. For it is no small matter to sin against the laws of God, as the period that follows will show." Here the author used a nice interplay of tenses to convey a heightened sense of incongruity. The aorist is used to survey at a glance the course of a past action from beginning to end (*perieschen, eschon*), while the imperfect expresses an action attempted and intended in the past (*ezēloun, ēthelon*). The hindsight juxtaposition of the tenses underlines the irony, and, at the same time, looks to the future punishment of the evil-doers (*dēlōsei*). The reflection at 2 Macc 5:17-20 both looks to the past when Heliodorus was repulsed and to the future restoration of the temple when God has been reconciled. The reflection at 2 Macc 6:12-17 claims that God has not abandoned his people, and it too points to the return of God's mercy. This forward-looking character of the reflections gives significance to the narrative of 2 Macc 4:1-7:42. In particular, the atoning quality of suffering as stressed in 2 Macc 6:12-17 colors the exemplary suffering of Eleazar and is explicit stated by the seventh brother as he prays:

> I, like my brothers, give up body and soul for the laws of my forefathers, calling upon God to show mercy speedily to our nation, and to lead you to confess, in trials and plagues, that he alone is God; and to stay through me and my brothers the wrath of the Almighty, which has justly fallen on our whole nation (2 Macc 7:37-38).[19]

This expectation is realized in the growing strength of Judas (2 Macc 8:4: "for the wrath of the Lord has turned to mercy") and particularly in the epiphanic victory over Nicanor (2 Macc 8:27: "as the Lord had begun to show them mercy"). Antiochus, too, confesses God's power on his death bed (2 Macc 9:11-17).

The role of the reflections is thus to explain the events of 2 Macc 4:1-7:42, and to highlight how the persecutions suffered bring about a reversal in the history of the Jews. The narrative of 2 Macc 4:1-7:42, through the reflections, becomes the black against which the white of the events of Heliodorus' repulsion in 2 Maccabees 3 and the victory over Nicanor in 2 Macca-

---

[19] S. Williams (*Jesus' Death as Saving Event* [Missoula: Scholars Press, 1975] 76-90) discusses whether the doctrine of vicarious atonement is present in 2 Maccabees. His conclusion is negative. Whatever the answer to this question, however, one must state that the deaths of the martyrs is a watershed in the narrative of 2 Maccabees, after which God's mercy abounds.

bees 8 shines out in sharper relief, as the time of wrath contrasts with the time of mercy. The reflections are interpreters of the narrative, and they underline the theme discerned in the analysis of 2 Maccabees 3: God is the defender and savior of his people, but only if they are sinless.

B. 2 Macc 8:1-10:9: The Restoration of the Temple:

After the description of the evils that came upon the Jews under Antiochus IV comes the tale of the elimination of those evils. First comes a major victory over the enemy, then the death of the arch-villain Antiochus IV, and finally the re-dedication of the temple.

(i) The defeat of Nicanor (2 Maccabees 8):

The narrative of the expedition of Nicanor is skillfully written at all levels. On the level of language, one notes that the middle voice of *prosanalegesthai* is attested in the Greek language so far known to us only at 2 Macc 8:19; the same is true of the active *oplologein tina* found at 2 Macc 8:27.31. At 2 Macc 8:35, *doxikē* is used instead of the more usual *endoxos*, and the author uses *skyla*, *laphra*, and *chrēmata* to give variety of expression in talking of booty won. The use of *diestēsato* at 2 Macc 8:10 is also unusual: in context, its meaning approaches that of "decided," i.e., by himself in opposition to the other advisors or to Ptolemy.[20] Another infrequent word used in this section of 2 Maccabees is *deilandrein* (2 Macc 8:13). Finally, the author shows himself well acquainted with Hellenistic terminology of battle accounts: *chreia* = military engagement (2 Macc 8:20; Plb. 1.84.7); *synagō* = enlist (2 Macc 8:1; D.S.19.91.5); *procheirizō* = appoint (2 Macc 8:9); *systēma* = body of soldiers (2 Macc 8:5; Plb. 1.81.11); *euandria* = abundance of men (2 Macc 8:7: Plu *Per* 19);[21] the use of a catch-word, *synthēma* (2 Macc 8:23), is also common in Greek literature.[22] Even the change from indirect to direct speech within the exhortation of Judas at 2 Macc 8:16-20 reflects the usage of Hellenistic historians.[23] At the lowest level of content structure, i.e., language, this chapter shows a knowledge of the terms used in Greek historiographical works and, by its use of rare words, aims at elevated style.

---

[20] This would require a new entry in Liddell and Scott.

[21] Not, as it is usually taken and as it means in 2 Macc 15:17, "valor." Philip is not worried about Judas' bravery, but by the fact that he is gathering such an effective fighting force. Cf. Plu *Per* 19; Xen *Mem* 3.3.12.

[22] Cf. the use of such catch-words in 1QM 3 and 4.

[23] P. Pédech, *La méthode historique de Polybe* (Paris: Société d'Édition "Les Belles Lettres," 1964) 280: "Dès le livre III Polybe adopte un procédé dont il fera un usage de plus en plus fréquent. Le discours commence au style indirect, puis après quelques phrases, il passe au style direct, comme si l'auteur entraîné par son sujet, préférait une exposition plus concrète et saisissante."

Much skill is also used in the telling of the narrative. It proceeds with ease and economy from the introduction of the problem confronting the Jews to its resolution in their favor. The account centers around one decisive battle, and the plans of the enemy are turned topsy-turvy. Nicanor had planned to sell the Jewish captives as slaves (2 Macc 8:10-11), but this slave money becomes part of the Jews' booty (2 Macc 8:25), and Nicanor himself is forced to flee as a slave (2 Macc 8:34-35). The Jews fight, ready to die for their laws and their country (2 Macc 8:21); this dedication to the laws is acted out in their observance of the sabbath (8:26-27), and their division of the spoils to those tortured and to the widows and orphans. Certain events, then, have been selected and highlighted by the author so that a dramatic unity is presented.

Within this account, where do the emphases lie? Certainly not on military maneuvers, nor on tactics, nor where the battle took place, nor how long the battle took: the battle description takes up half a verse. What a field day Polybius would have had in criticizing the author![24] What are emphasized by the author are: the help of God, the question of booty, and the fate of Nicanor.

The help of God is underlined throughout the narrative. In the opening paragraph of 2 Maccabees 8 which describes Judas' rise to power (8:1-7), both the prayer (8:2-4) and the genitive absolute phrase of 8:5b—*tēs orgēs tou kyriou eis eleon trapeisēs*—are not germane to a description of guerilla warfare.

> And they called upon the Lord to look upon the people who were oppressed by all men and to have pity on the sanctuary which had been profaned by the godless, and to have mercy on the city which was being ruined and would soon be leveled with the ground, and to hearken to the blood that cried to them, and to remember the lawless destruction of the innocent babies and the blasphemies uttered against his name, and to hate their wickedness. And as soon as Maccabeus got them organized, the heathen found him irresistible, for the wrath of the Lord now turned to mercy.

It is important for the author of 2 Maccabees to bring in how God's help was vitally necessary. The phrase of 8:5b connects with the reflection of 5:20 and the prayer of the seventh martyred brother at 7:37-38. It establishes the change from wrath to mercy brought about by the persecutions. God has been reconciled by the suffering. God's help in the upcoming battle is foreshadowed at 8:11 ("[Nicanor] . . . little expecting the judgement from the

---

[24] See Polybius on Timaeus, Ephorus, and Theopompus in 12.25, particularly 25 i.

Almighty that was to overtake him"), it is the theme of Judas' speech (8:16-20), and his battle signal, *theou boētheia* (8:23). The battle is won because God is the Jews' ally (8:24), the victors recognize this in their praise (8:27b) and their prayer (8:29), and the defeated Nicanor also confesses that the Jews have a champion (8:36: *hypermachos*) who makes them invulnerable.

The emphasis on the booty of the battle also leads one back to the theme of the help of God. First, the pursuit is stopped because of the reverence for the Sabbath, and so not as much booty is collected as might have been. Secondly, the booty is divided with proper provision being given to the tortured, the widows, and orphans. One can understand the reference to widows and orphans in this context following the regulations of Deut 14:29; 26:12, but whence comes the division of booty to the persecuted? Could *ēkismenois* refer here only to the wounded? In the LXX, outside these references in 2 Maccabees 8, the word and its derivatives are found only in 2, 3, and 4 Maccabees.[25] In all these instances, it means "to torture." The same is true of the usage in Josephus and Philo, where the sense is "to commit outrage against another";[26] this is particularly so in Philo's *In Flaccum* and *Ad Gaium* and in Josephus' *Jewish War*. Nowhere has *aikizomai* the meaning of "to wound in battle," but it means "to persecute." However, only in 2 Maccabees 8 is it stated that those who suffered persecution are given a share in the booty: why is this? From Num 31:27 and 1 Sam 30:21-25, one can see that booty should be equally divided between the fighters and the rest of the community. It is significant, however, that in 2 Maccabees 8 the ones mentioned are the *persecuted*, the widows and the orphans. The prayers of widows and orphans are sure to be heard by God (Exod 22:22). For the author of 2 Maccabees, the prayers of the persecuted have great power: their blood cries from the earth to be heard (2 Macc 8:3).[27] The martyrdoms help bring about the salvation of the people (2 Macc 7:37-38). In the author's reasoning, then, rightly do the persecuted share in the booty, for their sufferings have helped bring about the victory.

In this account of 2 Maccabees 8, the role of Nicanor is emphasized. This is part and parcel of the dramatic presentation of this event. As was seen above in a comparison of the battle in 2 Maccabees 8 and 1 Macc 3:38-4:25, the accent in 2 Maccabees 8 falls squarely on the personage of

---

[25] *Aikizomai*: 2 Macc 7:1.13.15; 3 Macc 5:42; 4 Macc 1:1; 6:16. *aikismos*: 2 Macc 8:17; 4 Macc 6:9; 7:4; 14:1; 15:19.

[26] *Aikizomai* is used metaphorically by Josephus in the context of doing harm to oneself through excessive grief (*Ant* 7.252; 8.325), and by Philo in the context of the senses outraging the faculty of reason (*De Post. Cain.* 184; cf. *De fuga* 121), but the sense of "committing outrage against another" is still present.

[27] For a discussion of "blood crying from the ground," see G. Vermes, "The Targumic Versions of Genesis IV 3-16," ALUOS 3 (1961-62) 81-114.

Nicanor and his fate. He it is who determines to sell the Jewish captives as slaves, and this becomes a significant factor in the story, where it is used to heighten dramatic irony.[28] The opposition lies between Nicanor, determined to humiliate his enemy, and the help of God given to the Jews. This opposition brings about Nicanor's fall, for it is God who causes such just deserts for the wicked.[29]

In sum, the account of the expedition of Nicanor in 2 Maccabees 8 provides a highly stylized version of the first major battle of the Jews after the Lord's wrath had turned to mercy. Whereas in 1 Maccabees this confrontation is but the third of four such confrontations which take place between the rise of Judas and the purification of the sanctuary, in 2 Maccabees it occupies center stage.[30] The emphasis is on the intervention of God on Israel's behalf. The finale sums up the purpose as Nicanor testifies that the Jews have a defender and that on this account they are invulnerable, because they follow the laws ordained by that defender. This proclamation strikingly echoes that of Heliodorus at 2 Macc 3:39 and also the final victory shout of the Jews at 2 Macc 15:34: "Blessings on him who has preserved his own dwelling from pollution."

The account is highly stylized, but what of the events narrated in 2 Macc 8:30-33? These accounts of other campaigns disrupt the concentration on Nicanor. Actors are introduced, e.g., Timothy, Bacchides, and Callisthenes, who are not prepared for in the preceding account. Where do these verses belong? Many commentators have sought to find a more suitable historical framework for the events: the answer is bound up with the problem of how many Timothys there are in 2 Maccabees. If one opts for two Timothys, one corresponding to the events of 2 Macc 10:24-38, the other to 2 Macc 12:1.10.18-25, then one can choose either location for the events in these verses. If one decides that only one Timothy is spoken of, then 2 Macc 8:30-33 will be located in the reshuffled other events which cluster around

---

[28] C. Habicht is wrong to deny irony at 2 Macc 8:35. *Euēmerein epi* means "successful," whereas Habicht would seem to separate off the prepositional phrase and translate: "succeeding well (i.e., being lucky to escape), while his army was destroyed." However, the irony is that Nicanor was successful in the destruction of his army. The reflection at 2 Macc 4:16-17, the description of Jason's assault on his fellow-citizens at 5:6, as well as the condemnation of Judas by Alcimus (14:6-10) all show the author capable of irony. The position of this ironic touch within these verses undermines the attempt of Bunge (*Untersuchungen*, 277-278) to rearrange the order of 2 Maccabees 8 so that originally the order would have been: 21-24; 34-35; 25-29. Such an arrangement robs the story of its literary climax!

[29] See chap. four.

[30] One wonders if the name "Nicanor" has been chosen by the author because of the recurrence in 2 Maccabees 15. The author has placed the first expedition of Lysias during the reign of Antiochus V Eupator. See below.

that name.[31] Whatever the answer to the historical problem, one has to admit that these verses have been well woven into the present texture of 2 Maccabees. 2 Macc 8:30-31 have been linked to the previous narrative by the repetition of the phrase "to the tortured, and the widows and orphans," as well as by the re-use of the unusual word *oplologein* at 8:31 after its use at 8:27. 8:32 attaches to 8:30-31 as it again deals with Timothy (8:30: *tois peri Timotheon kai Bakchidēn*; 8:32: *tōn peri Timotheon*).[32] 8:33 would have belonged to this cluster of events, and it also uses the "just deserts" theology, as the burners are burnt.[33] This complex of verses has been woven into the structure of 2 Maccabees, as they are referred to at 2 Macc 9:3 (*ta kata Nikanora kai tous peri Timotheon gegonota*) and at 2 Macc 10:24 (*Timotheos de ho proteron hēttētheis*). The epitomizer used these verses to signal perhaps that there were other campaigns at this time besides that of Nicanor as well as to draw the narrative of the death of Antiochus IV into relation with the defeat of Nicanor and the turning of God's anger into mercy.[34] How is this death described?

(ii) The Death of Antiochus IV (2 Maccabees 9):

The narrative describing the death of Antiochus IV is also highly stylized. All the stops are pulled out as the gruesome torments surrounding his disease are related with relish, and as the persecutor of the Jews is forced to submit and plea for mercy from the God he offended. This depiction fits well with stories of the deaths of scoffers against God.[35] To this account is added a letter, penned while Antiochus is in such death throes. The position of such a death-bed "testament" is a well-tried literary device: a parallel is furnished

---

[31] For a full discussion of the positions taken by scholars, see M. Zambelli, "La composizione," 272-278. Bunge (*Untersuchungen*, 291) retains the present separation of the two accounts of 2 Macc 10:24-38 and 12:18-25 and the present order, so he must maintain that there are two Timothys.

[32] Bunge (*Untersuchungen*, 280) leaves open the question of whether to read a proper name, *phylarchos*, or "cavalry commander," *phylarchēs*. However, he leans toward the latter (*Untersuchungen*, 282-283). Abel and Habicht take the rank rather than the name. Goldstein (*I Maccabees*, 296-297) maintains two Timothys, one of whom was a *strategos* (2 Macc 8:30; 12), the other was a *phylarch* (2 Macc 8:32; 10:24-37). He has not given the reasons for his text-critical decisions on 2 Macc 8:32. Further, Goldstein holds that the mention of Timothy at 2 Macc 9:3 is a "piece of stupidity," and that 10:24, *ho proteron hēttētheis* should be translated "the first (of the two bearing the name) to be defeated by the Jews." This is not correct, and very subjective.

[33] I read ἕν. For a discussion, see Katz, "The Text," 11. I agree with Bunge (*Untersuchungen*, 281) and Habicht that *patris* refers to the fatherland as such, as elsewhere in the narrative (4:1; 5:8.9.15; 8:21; 13:3.11.14; 14:18), and not to Jerusalem.

[34] Via 2 Macc 9:3.

[35] See W. Nestle, "Legenden vom Tod der Gottesverächter," *ARW* 33 (1936) 246-269. Examples abound in Lactantius' *De Mortibus Persecutorum*.

in the death scene of Alexander the Great in the account of Ps.-Callisthenes. Alexander, after being poisoned and attacked by hideous pains and almost unable to speak, spends a day writing his will and testament.[36] That such a literary device is used here coincides with the judgment that the letter is not authentic, although it may be modelled in some ways on official letters.[37] What is the role of this letter in 2 Maccabees? This question is neglected in the literature on 2 Maccabees. The letter gives no precise date. It is not locked into its context.[38] What, then, is its purpose? One cannot help being struck by the opening greeting: "To the esteemed Jewish citizens . . . " This high estimation of the Jews throughout the letter. At 2 Macc 9:21, the king remembers with affection their esteem and good will (*tēn timēn kai tēn eunoian*). The letter concerns the orderly transfer of power to Antiochus' heir, if anything should happen to him, and Antiochus places his trust *in the Jews* for the success of his transfer (2 Macc 9:25). He asks *the Jews* to continue their goodwill (*eunoian*) to him and his son (2 Macc 9:26). Throughout this letter the emphasis is unmistakable: the Jews are good and reliable citizens whom the king can trust. Such an apologetic purpose is found elsewhere in 2 Maccabees. It is not the Jews who start the conflicts, but subverters of the peace like Simon (3:4, 4:1), Jason (5:5), Antiochus (5:11.22), Gorgias (10:14), the surrounding governors (12:2), and Alcimus (14:3-10.26). When the Jews wish to live in peace, they are not allowed to (12:1-2). On the other hand, when cities do treat Jews favorably, as Scythopolis had done (12:29-30), Judas and his band do not molest them. Even non-Jews recognize the outrages done against the Jews, and show their respect for the victims: at an unjust murder of Onias (4:35) and of the envoys to Antiochus IV (4:49), the inhabitants of Antioch and Tyre respectively are indignant. This apologetic throughout 2 Maccabees must be related to the concern of all Hellenistic Jewry to show that Jews were not anti-social. Stories attributed to Posidonius of Apamea concerning the anti-social character of the Jews are examples of what the author of 2 Maccabees and his co-nationalists would have had to combat.[39]

---

[36] Ps.Callisthenes, *Historia Alexandri Magni* (ed. G. Kroll; Berlin: Weidmann, 1958) 2.32-33.

[37] This has been convincingly shown by C. Habicht in "Royal Documents in Maccabees II,"*Harvard Studies in Classical Philology* 80 (1976) 1-18, as well as in his commentary ad loc. Habicht suggests that the letter was modelled on a letter to the army, whose support would have been crucial in any change of leadership.

[38] Unless one wishes to hold that the hope of Antiochus of escaping the sickness, expressed in the letter at 9:22, is simply his putting on a good face in spite of his own convictions expressed in 9:18.

[39] See the remarks of Manetho, Hecataeus of Abdera, Posidonius of Apamea, and Apollonius Molon on the anti-social nature of the Jews. See the collection of M. Stern, *Greek*

In fine, the narrative of 2 Maccabees portrays the death of Antiochus IV as punishment for his blasphemous behavior towards the God of Israel,[40] and the letter attributed to the dying Antiochus underlines that his hubritic behavior, and not any anti-social hatred by the Jews, was the root of the persecution.

(iii) The Purification of the Temple (2 Macc 10:1-9):

The re-dedication of the temple is accomplished through God's aid. This factor is underscored by the providential circumstance that the purification takes place on the same day that the temple had been defiled.[41] In their prayer (2 Macc 10:4), the Jews ask that, if they sin in future, God would discipline them (*paideuesthai*) leniently by himself, and not hand them over to barbarous nations. This use of *paideuesthai* echoes the reflection of 2 Macc 6:12-17. The rededication of the temple is thus seen as the symbol that God's anger has indeed turned to mercy. The narrative of 2 Macc 8:1-10:8 is the response to the assault of evil described in 2 Macc 4:1-7:42.

That 2 Macc 8:1-10:8 is also a literary unit can be shown. As was noticed above, the account of Nicanor's defeat is linked to the account of Antiochus' death. But this account is also linked to the re-dedication of the temple. The conclusion of the account of Antiochus' death begins:

9:28: *ho men oun androphonos kai blasphēmos* . . .To what does this *men oun* refer? Most commentators have ignored this question. They have insisted, however, that 2 Macc 10:1-8 does not belong where it is,[42] and one must therefore infer that either the *men oun* does not have a correspondent, or that it refers to the *de* in 9:29: *parekomizeto de to sōma Philippos ho syntrophos autou hos* . . . In all other instances in 2 Maccabees where *men oun* occurs (2 Macc 3:22; 7:42; 10:22.28; 11:18.19), it is followed by *de*. One would therefore expect that this would be the case here. Does it therefore refer to 9:29? Against such a position, one must state that the emphatic position of the subject at the beginning in 9:28—*ho men oun androphonos kai blasphēmos*—finds its appropriate contrast at 10:1—*Makkabaios de kai hoi syn autọ*. 2 Macc 9:29 contains not a contrast to the blasphemer, but a

---

and Latin Authors on Jews and Judaism. Vol. I: From Herodotus to Plutarch (Jerusalem: Jerusalem Academic Press, 1974).

[40] 2 Macc 5:21: "thinking in his arrogance that he would make the land navigable and the sea traversable on foot." 2 Macc 7:19: "But you must not suppose that you will go unpunished for having attempted to fight against God (*theomachein epicheirēsas*)."

[41] For a collection of events that happened on the same day, see Aelian *Varia Historia* 2.25. Aelian relates that Alexander the Great is also said to have been born and to have died on the same day of the same month. Disasters cluster around the Ninth of Av in *m. Ta'an* 4:6; cf. Josephus *J.W.* 6.249-50.

[42] Abel, Schunck, Bunge, Habicht.

development of the story of the blasphemer's death, indicating what happened to his corpse. The contrast is between the account of Antiochus IV's death, and the events surrounding his opponent, Judas. Here, the *men oun* rounds off the old topic, while the *de* clause introduces the new one.[43] The two events of the death of Antiochus IV and the restoration are thus intertwined literarily to form the present structure of 2 Maccabees.

Such a conclusion has important consequences. As stated above, most commentators have held that 2 Macc 10:1-8 does not belong in its present position. This judgment is based on the fact that, at 2 Macc 10:9, one reads: "Such was the end of Antiochus, who was called Epiphanes." Since 2 Macc 10:1-8 does not speak of Antiochus IV, but of the purification of the temple, 10:9 must be re-located to 2 Maccabees 9. Such reasoning ignores the bond between 9:28 and 10:1. Should 10:9 then be placed after 9:27? But there Antiochus' death has not yet been recorded. In fact, commentators have not been alert to the fact that 10:9 is a purely transitional sentence which returns to the dynastic topos. The events of the reign of Antiochus IV have been recorded, it is now time to turn to those of his son. Once one concludes that 2 Macc 10:1-8 belong where they are and do not need to be re-located, one is spared the problem of deciding who would have re-located them. One no longer needs to do what Bunge did. He held that the author had re-located these verses, which originally stood immediately after the defeat of Nicanor in 2 Maccabees 8, and the author was forced to do so because he interpreted the prefixed letter of 2 Macc 1:10-17 to show that Antiochus IV died before the temple was restored.[44] For Bunge, Jason of Cyrene would originally have had the same order of events as 1 Maccabees, whereby Antiochus IV died after the purification of the temple, but the author changed this. Such reasoning is completely unnecessary. There has been no dislocation of text, and the present arrangement follows what is now known to be the correct historical order of events, with the death of Antiochus IV preceding the purification of the temple.

The narrative from 2 Macc 8:1-10:8 is thus a literary unit, which corresponds to the earlier unit of 4:1-7:42. The unit groups together the first battle victory, the death of the arch-villain, and the restoration of the temple. By such a grouping, the author has achieved a remarkable dramatic unity. Moving swiftly, God beat off Israel's enemies, destroyed the arch-antagonist Antiochus, and restored his defiled temple. It is appropriate that Antiochus, the main opponent of the Jews and the chief obstacle to the restoration of

43 J.D. Denniston, *The Greek Particles* (2nd ed.; Oxford: Clarendon Press, 1970) 472. For an example of a large distance separating the μὲν οὖν and δέ, see Philo *De Praemiis et Poenis* 1, 1-2 § 408.

44 Bunge, *Untersuchungen*, 279.

the temple, should die by God's hand before the restoration. In true gratitude, the Jews establish a festival to commemorate this unexpected deliverance. What a contrast to the narration of events 1 Maccabees. There the king also dies in a strange land of a sudden sickness brought on by news of Judas' victories (1 Macc 6:1-17), and he is forced to confess that the cause of his misfortunes was his improper treatment of the Jews. In 2 Maccabees, however, the news of Judas' victories only made Antiochus more furious, and he set out to stamp down and level the sanctuary completely, still vaunting his power (2 Macc 9:4.14). God is portrayed as actively defeating him (2 Macc 9:5-12). This is quite a distance from the sickness that overtakes Antiochus in the account of 1 Maccabees. In 2 Maccabees, Antiochus, not humbled at all by the news of Nicanor's defeat but still as arrogant as in his earlier pillage of the temple,[45] remains the arch-antagonist. How fitting that God's providential disposal of him should occur as he is on his way to destroy Jerusalem once for all. It is a highly dramatic account. Such a literary arrangement gives even greater weight to the joy of restoration.[46]

2 Macc 10:10-15:36: The Defense of the Temple:

After the temple has been restored, the narrative in 2 Maccabees is concerned with the repulse of further attacks upon it. Within this block of narrative, one notices the marked contrast between the rather condensed version of the many campaigns that occur in 2 Macc 10:14-13:26 and the more leisurely account of the expedition of Nicanor in 2 Macc 14-15. I shall deal first with the events narrated in 2 Macc 10:10-13:26, before dealing with those of 2 Macc 14-15.

A. 2 Macc 10:10-13:26.

After a discussion of dynastic changes and the appointment of Lysias over affairs (2 Macc 10:10-13), the narrative in 2 Macc 10:14-38 is concerned with skirmishes along the southern border (10:14-23) and in the vicinity of Yazer (2 Macc 10:24-38).[47] 2 Maccabees 11 deals not with an attack by a local governor but with the expedition of the main minister of the kingdom, Lysias, and the peace that was concluded at the end of this campaign. 2 Maccabees 12 opens with attacks on Jews along the coastal plain (12:3-9),

---

[45] Hyperēphania at 2 Macc 5:21; 9:7; hyperēphanōs at 9:4.

[46] Of course, it is also the historical order of events. For the literary side, cf. V. Propp, Morphology of the Folktale (2nd ed.; Austin/London: University of Texas Press, 1973): Function I; The Villain is Defeated; Function K: The Initial Misfortune or Lack is Liquidated.

[47] On the comparison with the narrative of 1 Macc 5:8, one must read Yazer (with Grimm, Niese, Kolbe, and recently Goldstein, 1 Maccabees, 296) as against the manuscript tradition which reads γαζαρα, and which has been defended by Abel and Habicht.

an attack by Arabs (12:10-12) as Judas and his party were on their way towards Transjordan, where various battles and sieges take place (12:12-28). From there, the army marched back to Jerusalem (12:29-31), and then on to the south against Gorgias (12:32-45). 2 Maccabees 13 deals with a major expedition under the command of Lysias and Antiochus V Eupator, and ends with a peace treaty.

One can see how the author has arranged his material: local attacks followed by a major expedition and peace. Such is not the historical order of the events. The situation has been clarified by the recent close examination of the documents preserved in 2 Macc 11:17-38. The letters are recognized as genuine documents.[48] However, their present order and framework are faulty. The documents are as follows:

1. (2 Macc 11:17-21)
   Lysias sends greeting to the Jewish people. Your emissaries John and Absalom have presented the accompanying petition and asked about the matters set forth in it. So I informed the king of the matters that needed to be laid before him, but what was within my competence I have agreed to.[49] If then you continue your loyalty to the government, I will endeavor to further your interests in the future. About the details of these matters, I have ordered these men and my representatives to confer with you. Goodbye. The hundred and forty-eighth year, Dioscorinthius twenty-fourth.

2. (2 Macc 11:22-26)
   King Antiochus sends greeting to his brother Lysias. Now that our father has departed to the gods, we desire the subjects of the kingdom to be unmolested and to busy themselves with their own affairs. As we have heard that the Jews will not agree to our father's policy of making them adopt Greek practices, but prefer their own customs, we wish this nation also to be undisturbed, and our decision is that their temple be returned to them, and that they follow their ancestral customs. Please send messengers to them therefore, and give them assurances, so that they may know our purpose and be of good cheer, and contentedly go about the conduct of their affairs.

3. (2 Macc 11:27-33)
   King Antiochus sends greeting to the Jewish senate and to the rest of the Jews. If you are well, it is what we desire; we too are well. Menelaus has informed us that you want to go home and look after

---

[48] See C. Habicht, "Royal Documents."

[49] I have read συνεχώρησα at 2 Macc 11:18 with most of the manuscripts and with Abel and Habicht and most editors. Hanhart reads συνεχώρησεν, based on the Syriac.

your own affairs. Therefore those who go home by the thirtieth of Xanthicus will have our assurance that the Jews can fearlessly enjoy their own food and laws, as before; and none of them shall be molested in any way for what he may have ignorantly done. I have sent Menelaus also to cheer you. Goodbye. The hundred and forty-eight year, Xanthicus fifteenth.

4. (2 Macc 11:34-38)

Quintus Memmius and Titus Manius, envoys of the Romans, send greeting to the Jewish people. With regard to what Lysias, the king's relative, has granted you, we also give our approval. But as to the matters which he decided should be referred to the king, as soon as you have considered the matter, send us word, so that we may take proper action. For we are going to Antioch; so make haste and send men to us, so that we also may know what your intentions are. Goodbye. The hundred and forty-eight year, Xanthicus fifteen.

The year dates in the first, third, and fourth letters are not difficult to accept, but the same is not true of the month dates. Dioscorinthius of the first letter remains obscure.[50] The third and fourth letters could not have been written on the same day of the same year, for they presuppose different circumstances: the fourth must be prior to a decision of a king, the third is a decision of a king. Within the third letter, a difficulty arises between the date for the end of the amnesty, the 30th Xanthicus, and the date of the letter, the 15th Xanthicus.[51] This is much too short a time for an amnesty. The date within the letter would seem more reliable than that at the end of the letter, given the other difficulties surrounding these month data. While, therefore the year seems reliable for the first, third, and fourth letters, no further precision can be gained as to the month.

In 2 Maccabees 11, one receives the impression that all the letters come from the reign of Antiochus V. Such is not the case. In 148 of the Seleucid era, Antiochus IV was still reigning. However, the second letter clearly dates from the reign of Antiochus V. C. Habicht has convincingly demonstrated the correct historical framework for these letters.[52] The third letter in the series was the response of Antiochus IV to a mission of Menelaus. It took place sometime before the 30th Xanthicus, 148 Sel. i.e., before the end of

---

[50] La^B: Διὸς Κορινθίου; La^XV(-L): dioscori; La^L: dioscordi; La^PV:L: dioscoridi(s); La^M: deoscolori. Habicht suggests that the first Macedonian month Δίου is more likely than the fifth Δύστρου or the eighth Δαισίου, but gives no sure solution.

[51] Tcherikover (*Hellenistic Civilisation*, 219) takes the dates as correct, and sees the fortnight given as a ruse on the part of the government to condemn those who did not comply with this impossible timetable. Emendation seems preferable.

[52] C. Habicht, *2 Makkabäerbuch*, 177-185; "Royal Documents."

March, 164 B.C.E. Menelaus' mission was to bring an end to the revolt by the revocation of the previous decrees outlawing the practice of the Jewish religion. By such a revocation, it was hoped that the uprising would come to an end by peaceful means. When this failed, and Judas and his band did not disperse to their homes by the time for the end of the amnesty program, the expedition of Lysias became necessary to restore order. Lysias too failed to subdue the rebels, and entered into peace negotiations with Judas. To these negotiations belong the first and fourth letters. These proposals of Lysias were never answered, however, for Antiochus IV died while on his northern expedition without rendering a decision.[53] On his accession to the throne, Antiochus V granted amnesty to his rebellious subjects, a gesture customary at the beginning of a reign. This amnesty is contained in the second letter.

What could have broken this amnesty achieved at the beginning of the reign of Antiochus V? M. Zambelli has suggested that the first campaign of Lysias through the south[54] had shown to Judas the necessity of blockading this southern flank. Hence he undertook a series of measures designed to block off this approach: he fortified Bethsur and other southern forts, and there was a series of skirmishes in Idumea. These confrontations, combined with the battles against Timothy and the coastal towns, brought about the second intervention of Lysias accompanied by Antiochus V. Following this reconstruction, the events narrated in 2 Macc 10:14-38 (and 8:30-33) should be placed with those of 2 Maccabees 12. Such an arrangement would also solve the difficulty of the number of Timothys, for the death of 10:37 would come after the event of 12:2.10-24, where a Timothy reappears.[55] Zambelli would also hold that the court changes mentioned in 2 Macc 10:10-13 would have occurred prior to the second campaign of Lysias, i.e., before the narrative of 2 Macc 13:1.[56]

If one accepts this reconstruction of the historical events, one can see how the author has skillfully arranged the disparate material. As noted above, Antiochus IV is presented throughout the narrative of 2 Maccabees 5-9 as the arch-antagonist of the Jews who does not repent of his folly until he is brought to his last breath. Such a villain could not have proposed the restoration of Jewish religion as proposed in the third letter. Therefore, the

---

[53] This is opposed to the view represented by Tcherikover (*Hellenistic Civilisation*, 215) that the letter of 2 Macc 11:27-33 was the response to the letters of 11:16-21 and 11:34-38. T. Liebmann-Frankfort makes a strong case that the letter of the Roman envoys was written after the death of Antiochus IV and that the Romans were trying to pressure the young Antiochus V. ("Rome et le conflict judéo-syrien [164-161 avant notre ère]," *L'Antiquité Classique* 38 [1969] 106-107.)

[54] M. Zambelli, "La Composizione," 267-268.

[55] M. Zambelli, "La Composizione," 277-278.

[56] M. Zambelli, "La Composizione," 278-279.

letter must belong to the reign of Antiochus V. One should note that 1 Maccabees also does not allow for such an amnesty under Antiochus IV, who only repents of his dealings towards the Jews on his deathbed (1 Macc 6:1-17). Such an attitude is also evident in the account of the first campaign of Lysias in 1 Macc 4:28-35 which, in opposition to other battle accounts in 1 Maccabees, is told in very general terms as though the author knew no specific details. Peace initiatives under Antiochus IV are not considered in either 1 or 2 Maccabees. Once this is taken as granted, with the peace initiatives of the letters occurring under Antiochus V, then the campaigns of Lysias must also be arranged during this reign. Thus, with two campaigns of Lysias falling in the reign of Eupator, the author has so arranged his material that local battles occur before each major campaign.[57] Minor campaigns are followed by a major campaign and then peace. Such an arrangement gives a nice balanced structure.

The reconstruction of the process of the historical events was forced by the recognition of the reliability of the documents in 2 Macc 11:17-38. They are presently found in the wrong historical context and in the wrong order, and one is faced with the problem of why they are found in the epitome at all. The author has not hesitated to leave huge gaps in his narration of events; why, therefore, did he bother to supply the text of these letters? The answer would seem to lie in their accord with the apologetic purpose spoken of above in conjunction with the letter of 2 Macc 9:18-27. These letters show that all the Jews want to do is live according to the customs of their forefathers, to follow their own way of life and laws (2 Macc 11:24-25.30-31). The Jews are not, therefore, anti-social and haters of other nations, for they enter into diplomatic communication with the Romans (11:34-38)—they simply wish to follow their ancestral laws. Such an apologetic purpose is important in this section which deals with so many campaigns against other peoples. The author underlines that the Jews wish peace, but that others would not let them alone (12:1-2). The attempt of Ptolemy to deal justly with the Jews is foiled by hostile courtiers (10:10-13). The diplomatic relations with the Romans and the friendly attitude towards the Scythopolitans belie any anti-social charges or accusations of hatred against other races.[58]

---

[57] The selection of which campaigns to place in each section may have followed name usage: ὁ Μακκαβαῖος in 10-11, Ἰούδας in 12-13. See above pp. 16-17.

[58] One would also have to consider whether such a collection of documents in fact constituted a legal claim by the Jews to some special status, and this would be tied in with the view one took of the *Acta pro Iudaeis* in Josephus. For a recent discussion of the Josephus material, see H.R. Moehring, "The *Acta pro Judaeis* in the *Antiquities* of Flavius Josephus: A Study in Hellenistic and Modern Apologetic Historiography," *Christianity, Judaism and Other Greco-Roman Cults* (ed. J. Neusner; Festschrift M. Smith; Leiden: Brill, 1975) 3.124-158. For a discussion of the Persian background for the penchant of Jewish historians to quote

Finally, one should note in these campaigns the insistence of the theme that all victories are accomplished by the help of God. In some campaigns, it is simply stated that Judas or the Israelites invoked God's help (the campaign against the Idumeans, 10:14-23; against Joppa and Jamnia, 12:3-9; against Ephron, 12:27-28; against Gorgias, 12:32-37); in others, the Jews win by the help or protection of God (against the Arabs, 12:10-12; against Caspin, 12:13-16; against Lysias, 13:19-17); in two campaigns, visible epiphanies are described (against Timothy, 10:24-38; against Lysias, 11:1-14). All these campaign accounts are miniatures of the battles described in larger extent in 2 Maccabees 8 and 15. This is particularly true of the campaigns where visible epiphanies occur, as the antithesis between the Jewish forces and the forces of the enemy is heightened: the enemy commanders put their trust in their arms (10:28; 11:4), whereas Judas and his followers trust the Lord (10:28; 11:9-10). In the battle against Lysias, the enemy commander recognizes, as Heliodorus and Nicanor had done before him, the invincibility of the Jews with God as their champion. Emphasis remains on the help of God extended to protect his people.

B. 2 Macc 14:1-15:36

After the series of minor and major campaigns followed by peace treaties comes the final campaign in 2 Maccabees against the holy temple and its territory.

The first segment of the account, 2 Macc 14:1-25 gives the reason for the renewal of hostilities. The cause is the ambition of Alcimus, a former high-priest who was on opposite sides to Judas and his followers.[59] Alcimus denounces the Jews under Judas for precisely the opposite of what the rest of the narrative is trying to prove: Alcimus says that it is the Jews "who keep the war alive (*polemotrophousi*), and stir up sedition (*stasiazousin*), and will not let the kingdom enjoy stability (*ouk eōntes tēn basileian eustatheias tychein*) . . . for as long as Judas remains alive, the state will never be able to enjoy peace (*adunaton eirēnēs tychein ta pragmata*)" (2 Macc 14:6-10). This is exactly the reverse of how the author of 2 Maccabees describes the events. After the removal of Ptolemy Macron who had tried to act justly towards the Jews (2 Macc 10:10-13), the author narrates that it was Gorgias, the military commander of the region, who kept up the continual state of war

---

documents, see A. Momigliano, "Eastern Elements in Post-Exilic Jewish, and Greek, Historiography," *Essays in Ancient and Modern Historiography* (Middleton, CT: Wesleyan University Press, 1977) 31-33.

[59] Alcimus is brought unexpectedly into the narrative, and no mention has been made previously of Menelaus' successor.

with the Jews (*epolemotrophei*); outside of 2 Macc 10:14.15; 14:6, the verb is not found. As to Alcimus' complaint that Judas prevented the country from obtaining stability, the author has stated that it is the local military commanders who will not allow the Jews to live in peace and quiet (2 Macc 12:2: *ouk eiōn autous eustathein kai ta tēs hesychias agein*). The similarity of language is striking. This charge of Alcimus is, in fact, belied by the subsequent outcome of the expedition of Nicanor: without bloodshed agreement is reached, and Judas married, settled down, and led a normal life (*egamēsen, eustathēsen, ekoinōnēse biou*) (2 Macc 14:18-25).

The final charge of Alcimus, that the state will never enjoy peace as long as Judas remains alive (14:10), parallels the charge made by Onias III against the original troublemaker, Simon (2 Macc 4:6). It is doubly ironic as the two high-priests Onias and Alcimus represent two totally different viewpoints: while Alcimus had polluted himself of his own accord in the time of trouble (2 Macc 14:3), Onias was the embodiment of observance of the law (2 Macc 3:1). The accusation that the Jews are disturbers of the peace in a realm and the subsequent denial by the events themselves is a theme found elsewhere in Hellenistic Jewish literature. In the letter of Artaxerxes in the Greek Esther, one finds the same accusation at 3:13:

> Understanding therefore that this nation, and it alone, stands in constant opposition to all men, perversely following a strange manner of life and laws, and ill-disposed towards our administration, doing all the harm it can, so that our rule may not enjoy stability (*pros to mē tēn basileian eustatheias tynchanein*), we have decreed . . . so that they who all along have been disaffected may in a single day go down through violence to Hades, and leave our government stable and undisturbed in the future (*eustathē kai ataracha*).

This accusation has been brought forward by Haman, and is proved false (Esther 8). In 3 Maccabees, Ptolemy uses the same language to plot his campaign against the Jews. At 3 Macc 3:26 he writes: "When these (the Jews) have been punished as a body, we anticipate that our government will be perfectly established for all future time in a stable and excellent state (*hēmin ta pragmata en eustatheiạ kai tẹ beltistẹ diathesei katastathēsesthai*)." When Ptolemy is forced to repent of his folly, he orders: "Set free the children of the Almighty and heavenly living God, who from the days of our ancestors until now has conferred upon our estate unimpaired stability and glory (*aparapodiston meta doxēs eustatheian parechei tois hēmeterois pragmasin*)" (3 Macc 6:28). In his final letter revoking his earlier decisions, Ptolemy excuses his former actions by declaring that evil friends had so persuaded him, by urging that "our state will never be stable, because of the ill-will the Jews bear all nations (*mēpote eustathēsein ta pragmata hēmōn di'hēn echou-*

sin outoi pros ta panta ethnē dysmeneian)" (3 Macc 7:4). Such notions are false, writes Ptolemy: "Because we knew of a surety that God in heaven protects the Jews, being their ally always as a father to his children, and because we took account of the firm good will, like a friend's, which they had for us and our forebears, we have justly absolved them of all blame on every account" (3 Macc 7:6-7). In all these cases, charges brought against the Jews prove false. This theme is also found in 2 Macc 14:28 and 15:10: Nicanor is annoyed because he had to break the treaty with Judas, even though Judas had done no wrong; at 15:10, Judas reminds his troops of the perfidy of the heathen and how they had broken their oaths. Again, the Jews did not seek battle; it was forced on them.

This whole segment, then, reveals that polemic which was uncovered in the use of the letters in 2 Macc 9:18-27; 11:16-38—a polemic which attempted to disprove charges of anti-social behavior levelled against the Jews.

The following segment of the account, 14:26-15:5, depicts the change in Nicanor as he becomes the adversary of the Jews.[60] At Alcimus' instigation, the king orders Nicanor to imprison Judas. Judas escapes, and the first act of Nicanor is to threaten the temple (14:31-36). Since Judas had escaped his hands, he tries to capture Rhazis, but Rhazis dies rather than be a prisoner (14:37-46). Nicanor's final stratagem to catch Judas, to make use of the Sabbath rest and attack the Jews unawares (15:1-5), fails.

In the first episode (14:31-36), Nicanor disregards the right of asylum and threatens to level the precinct, as Antiochus IV had threatened.[61] Furthermore, Nicanor threatens to build a temple to Dionysus on that very spot. This is a frontal attack on the God of Israel. In response to it, the priests pray: "Keep undefiled forever this house so lately purified (*diatērēson eis aiōna amianton tonde ton prosphatōs kekatharismenon oikon)*" (14:36). This prayer finds its echo in the acclamation of the Jews after they have defeated Nicanor: "Blessed be he who has kept his own place from being defiled (*Eulogetos ho diatērēsas ton heautou topon amianton)*" (15:34). The

---

[60] There is no reason to regard the friendly attitude of Nicanor towards Judas as purely a literary device, as W. Richnow does: "Diese Episode scheint hier nicht um der historischen Wahrheit willen geschildert zu sein, sondern ein Kompositionselement darzustellen; man wird sie den 'romanhaften' Erfindungen unseres Autors zurechnen dürfen, die die Handlung beleben sollen" ("Untersuchungen," 154). Richnow does not at all consider the problems inherent in the picture of a hostile Nicanor in 1 Macc 7:26-30. The theme of the treacherous dealings of the enemy had already been applied to the acts of Bacchides and Alcimus at 1 Macc 7:10.16-18, and is simply re-applied to Nicanor at 1 Macc 1:27. Richnow has simply not taken account of the many problems inherent in the account of 1 Maccabees 7. Cf. W. Mölleken, "Geschichtsklitterung im I. Makkabäerbuch (Wann wurde Alkimos Hoherpriester?)," *ZAW* 65 (1953) 205-228. One should not capitulate entirely to the account of 1 Maccabees, as Richnow does.

[61] The language of the threats of Antiochus IV and Nicanor against the temple is very similar: 2 Macc 9:14: *isopedon poiēsai*; 14:33: *eis pedion poiēsō*.

episode in 2 Maccabees pits Nicanor against the God of Israel. In this, it differs from the acount in 1 Macc 7:33-38, where the threat to turn the temple into a temple of Dionysus is not found, nor the close verbal connection between the prayer of the priests at this threat and the final outcome of the battle.

In the Rhazis episode (14:37-36), Nicanor is depicted as venting his frustration on an innocent victim. "And Nicanor, wishing to show the enmity he felt for the Jews, sent more than five hundred soldiers to arrest him; for he thought that in arresting him, he would be doing them an injury." Rhazis is condemned because he loves his fellow-countrymen; Nicanor shows his enmity (*dysmeneia*) towards the Jews. Again, it is not the Jews who should be convicted of hatred for other races, but conversely.[62]

In the episode of 2 Macc 15:1-5, Nicanor again challenges the authority of God. In opposition to God's command to respect the Sabbath, a command given by one who is *en ouranō dynastēs*, Nicanor disregards it because he is *dynastēs epi tēs gēs*. It is a clear challenge against the God of Israel. Throughout 2 Macc 14:26-15:4, Nicanor stands forth as the challenger to the God of Israel, both in his contempt for God's laws and temple as in his enmity towards God's own people.

The battle is described in 15:6-36. It is to this that the narrative of 14:1-15:5 has been leading. The account is not situated geographically, as it is in 1 Macc 7:39-40. However, the impression given is that the confrontation took place in the vicinity of Jerusalem: "And those who were left in the city felt no slight distress, for they were anxious about the encounter in the open" (15:19). By the contrast between those in the city and those outside it, one imagines the battle to be taking place within view of the city. What is certain is that the battle will decide who will hold Jerusalem (15:17.37).[63]

The pre-battle preparations of the two forces are stongly contrasted throughout the account. Nicanor is full of haughtiness (15:6), while Judas recalls the help of God (15:7-16). The enemy's force draws itself up in battle array (15:20),[64] while Judas prays for help (15:21-24). Nicanor and his men advance with trumpets and battle-songs (15:25), Judas and his men with prayers (15:26). The antithesis is shaiply drawn.

The pre-battle activities of the Jews are developed in detail. Two aspects of that development are impoitant. First, one should note the similarities to

<hr />

[62] See above, pp. 60-61.

[63] One must of course remember that the author disregards the presence of the enemy force in the Akra, except for the fleeting reference at 2 Macc 15:31.

[64] The context of 2 Macc 15:20 requires that *symmeignymi* have the meaning of "join forces with" (as in Thuc 2.31), and not that of "join battle with." The enemy forces were grouping together and forming battle positions.

the language of holy war. a) Judas exhorts his men not to fear the attack of the heathen, but to wait for the victory which would come from the Almighty (15:8). This is a constant exhortation in accounts of holy war: Moses exhorts his followers before the passage to the Red Sea when Pharaoh draws near: "Fear not, stand firm, and see the salvation of the Lord, which he will work for you today" (Exod 14:13). Joshua exhorts his men similarly: "Do not fear or be dismayed; be strong and of good courage; for thus the Lord will do to all your enemies against whom you fight" (Josh 10:25; cf. 8:1).[65] b) Corresponding to this imbued courage of the Jews is the call for lack of steadfastness on the part of Israel's enemies. Judas prays that God send forth a good angel to bring fear and terror before them (15:23-24). This is the language of Exod 15:16: "Terror and dread fall upon them" (cf. Deut 2:25; 11:25).[66] c) In descriptions of holy war, a war shout often opens the battle. At Judg 7:19-20, Gideon and his men blow the trumpets and smash jars and cry out, "A sword for the Lord and for Gideon!"[67] At 2 Chr 20:1-30, this war shout is replaced by liturgical singing, as in the War Scroll at Qumran.[68] Something similar happens at 2 Macc 15:26: in opposition to the heathens advancing with their battle songs, the Jews approach praying aloud. d) Finally, in 2 Macc 15:27, the Jews win by God's epiphany,[69] and members of Nicanor's body are hung on the Jerusalem walls as a sign of the Lord's help.

The same kind of language is also found in 2 Maccabees 8: the exhortation by Judas to his men not to be panic-stricken by the enemy or to fear them (8:16-17). God is the ally of the Jews, and their dependence on him is understood by their observance of the Sabbath command and by the way the booty is divided.

The second aspect to be noted in the pre-battle activities of the Jews in 2 Maccabees 15 is that of divine help promised in a dream through the giving of a divine weapon, a sword, to the hero (2 Macc 15:12-16). Judas tells this dream in a pre-battle speech.[70] In this dream, two elements are intertwined, that of the promise of divine aid and that of the giving of special weapons to the hero. Promises of divine aid are frequent in all literature. In the cylinder texts which record the campaigns of Assurbanipal, the king tells of the help

---

[65] Cf. G. von Rad, *Der heilige Krieg im alten Israel* (4th ed.; Göttingen: Vandenhoeck & Ruprecht, 1965) 9-10.

[66] G. von Rad, *Der heilige Krieg*, 10-11.

[67] G. von Rad, *Der heilige Krieg*, 11.

[68] G. von Rad, *Der heilige Krieg*, 80-81.

[69] I agree with Bunge (*Untersuchungen*, 260, n. 126) that *epiphaneia* at 2 Macc 15:27 should be given full force because of its use throughout the book (2:21; 3:24; 5:4; 12:22; 14:15).

[70] For the delight of Greek historians in pre-battle speeches, see P. Pédech, *La Méthode*, 254-256.

given to him by Ishtar during the seventh campaign.[71] When Assurbanipal hears of the preparations for battle which Teuman, king of Elam, is making against him, he repairs to the temple of Ishtar and prays for help. Ishtar answers his prayer. That same night, the goddess appears to a seer and stands with a bow and a sword unsheathed for battle. In the vision, the goddess spoke to Assurbanipal and promised to be with him in the midst of the battle. The king trusts this oracle, goes out to war, and defeats Teuman. Polybius seems to report an almost cynical use of such dream encouragements.[72] Polybius records that Scipio, in his speech to the soldiers before the taking of New Carthage, spurred on his men. Scipio had spent months planning the assault and examining the approaches to the town; he had developed a strategy which made use of the quickly ebbing and flowing tidal wave. In his speech, Scipio encouraged his men by outlining his detailed calculations, by promising gold coins if they succeeded, and by recounting a dream in which Neptune had appeared to him to suggest the plan and to promise help in its execution. This is the first time Neptune has been mentioned in the account, but the soldiers believe it and follow the plan. Such examples of divine helpers abound.[73]

The second element in Judas' dream is the giving of a sword. The giving of special weapons to a hero is also a found motif, particularly in highly mythological epics and less monumental folk literature. In the *Enuma Elish*, Marduk is taught the power of magic by the gods so that he might destroy Tiamat. With these gifts, Marduk goes out to battle and subdues Tiamat.[74] In a similar cosmogonic epic, the cycle of Baʿl and ʿAnat, Baʿl overcomes Yamm through clubs which were fashioned for him by Kotar, craftsman of the gods.[75] Within heroic epics, one thinks of the Arthurian sword. Achilles, too, is given special weapons to fight Hector, weapons worked by Hephaistos.[76] In non-Homeric legends about Troy, the city could not be taken except by the weapons of Heracles. So Philoctetes, to whom the weapons had been bequeathed, must be brought from the island of Lemnos to accomplish this task.[77] Within folk-tale literature, the giving of special weapons is often a key motif.[78] The giving of magical instruments which assure success in combat is,

---

[71] Rassam Cylinder B, col. V, 52f., as published in D.D. Luckenbill, *Ancient Records of Assyria and Babylonia* (rep.; New York: Greenwood Press, 1968) 2.332, no. 861.

[72] Plb 10. 11.5-8.

[73] F. Pfister, art. "Epiphanie," PW, Supplementband 4.227-297.

[74] IV.19-32.

[75] CTA 2.4.11-15.

[76] *Iliad*, 18.428-19.23.

[77] Cf. Sophocles, *Philoctetes* 69; 1434-1435.

[78] S. Thompson, *Motif-index of Folk-literature* (Bloomington: Univ. of Indiana, 1955-59) D 1000.

in fact, expected in the larger-than-life epic or folk-tale context. These weapons have a reality of their own on the meta-historical plane of myth or tale. But what happens when this rather stylized mythic motif is put in the context of a story which claims to narrate history, i.e., non-mythic reality? The meta-historical motif is brought to the historical plane by means of the dream. Dreams are liminal events in which the link between the human and the divine plane occurs. That a divine being should offer special divine weapons to a hero during a dream is a special way by which divine beings give assurance of victory. This motif of the assurance of victory through the giving of a sword is found in the stele celebrating Marniptah's victory over the Libyans. When news of the Libyan aggression is brought to Marniptah, the Pharaoh upbraids his followers for their fears and encourages them to go out to battle. The army marches out. Ptah appears to Marniptah in a dream, gives him a sword, and tells him to banish the fearful heart from him. Amon-Re goes with the army, and they win a great victory.[79] The role of the motif in this victory stele in the Karnak temple strikingly parallels the role of the motif in 2 Macc 15:11-16. In 2 Maccabees, the motif is woven into a speech of Judas in accordance with the delight of Greek historians in pre-battle speeches, but it remains a divine assurance of victory.[80]

The use of the language of holy war in the account of the battle in 2 Maccabees 15 as well as the presence of the motif of divine assurance of victory through the giving, in a dream, of a weapon of war to the hero point to the attempt by the author to depict the battle as a clash between the God of Israel and his enemies. This aspect is even more pronounced in the finale to the battle, as the soldiers march to Jerusalem. There, gathered around God's altar, they hold an almost liturgical celebration of the victory.[81] The element of theomachy is underscored by the pinning to the walls of Nicanor's

---

[79] As published in J.H. Breasted, *Ancient Records of Egypt* (Chicago: Univ. of Chicago Press. 1906) 3, nos. 574-592, pp. 241-252. The motif of the god giving a sword to Pharaoh is also found in the Israel stele, the Cairo column (Breasted, *Ancient Records*, 2, no. 594), and the Athribis stele on which a relief depicts Marniptah receiving a sword from Amon-Re (Breasted, *Ancient Records*, III, no. 597).

[80] Bunge (*Untersuchungen*, 259-260) has completely overlooked this aspect of the presentation, and states that the dream of Judas (2 Macc 15:11b-16) is intrusive to the account. He offers no literary reasons for his rejection, but objects that the giving of a sword belongs to the beginning of a man's career, not to an event that occurs a month before his death. Bunge would relate this vision of 2 Macc 15:11b-16 to the episode in 1 Macc 3:11 where Judas, in his first campaign, gained possession of the sword of Apollonius and used it for the rest of his life. Such reasoning of Bunge's overlooks the literary significance of the vision as a divine assurance of victory in the coming battle.

[81] One could note similarities to the pattern of Victory Enthronement as outlined by Paul D. Hanson, "Zechariah 9 and the Recapitulation of an Ancient Ritual Pattern," *JBL* 92 (1973) 37-59.

blasphemous hand and head, and by giving his tongue to the birds, in reprisal for his actions at 14:31-33, where he had stretched out his hand against the holy temple and spoken arrogantly. The blasphemer is justly rewarded.

Conclusion:

Our analysis has revealed a three-fold structure underpinning the narrative of 2 Maccabees: 2 Maccabees 3; 4:1-10:9; 10:10-15:36. All three sections are concerned with attacks on the Jerusalem temple and the defense of that temple. In the first section, the attack failed because the laws of God were observed (2 Macc 3:1). In the second section, the sins of the people brought on the disasters under Antiochus IV; he in his pride oversteps the mark, however, by his cruel persecutions. When the anger of the Lord turns to mercy through the sufferings of the martyrs, Antiochus' forces are defeated and he himself punished and killed, while the temple is restored. In the final section, further attacks on the temple territory are turned back through God's help, which was especially present in the victory over Nicanor, and from which time the temple is in the hands of the Jews (2 Macc 15:37). Throughout the narrative, then, the concern is to glorify the defense of the temple and its territory by its patron deity.

This three-fold structure is confirmed by arguments from linguiştic repetition. The language used to describe the decision to institute a feast at the end of the second and third sections of the narrative is almost identical:

10:8 : ἐδογμάτισαν δὲ μετὰ κοινοῦ προστάγματος καὶ ψηφίσματος
15:38: ἐδογμάτισαν δὲ πάντες μετὰ κοινοῦ ψηφίσματος

Such a repetition points to an intention to structure the narrative in some way around the feasts of purification and the day of Nicanor. Similar repetition is found in the rubrics used at:

3:40: καὶ τὰ μὲν κατὰ Ἡλιόδωρον καὶ τὴν τοῦ γαζοφυλακίου τήρησιν οὕτως ἐχώρησεν
7:42: Τὰ μὲν οὖν περὶ τοὺς σπλαγχνισμοὺς καὶ τὰς ὑπερβαλλούσας αἰκίας ἐπὶ τοσοῦτον δεδηλώσθω
10:9 : Καὶ τὰ μὲν τῆς Ἀντιόχου τοῦ προσαγορευθέντος Ἐπιφανοῦς τελευτῆς οὕτως εἶχεν
13:26: οὕτως τὰ τοῦ βασιλέως τῆς ἐφόδου καὶ τῆς ἀναζυγῆς ἐχώρησεν
15:37: Τῶν οὖν κατὰ Νικάνορα χωρησάντων οὕτως . . .

Here too an intention to structure is present.[82] The rubric at 3:40 ends a self-contained event, as do those at 10:9 and 15:37. Such is not the case, however, at 7:42 and 13:26. The persecutions, summed up in 7:42, lead on to the victories of the Jews. The rubric at 13:26 concludes the events under Eupator's reign and gives slight pause to the narrative, but does not stop it. These rubrics at 7:42 and 13:26 have emerged as markers of the narrative, but not as major structural elements. Such an analysis confirms the view that the author intends to recount major victories, told from the point of view of a devotee of the God of Israel. This intention had already been stated in the prologue to the work, when the author said that he would recount the epiphanies by which the enemies of Israel were driven out of the land. (2:21)

Besides uncovering this major emphasis reflected in the structure of the work, the analysis has also brought to light another important theme within the work. This theme is the defense of the Jews against attacks that they are anti-social and hate other races.[83] The theme is not only found in the insistence that it was not the Jews but their enemies who started hostilities, but also accounts for the use of letters in this epitome.

---

[82] The importance of these concluding rubrics was noticed by Büchler (*Tobiaden und Oniaden*, 325) and Arenhoevel (*Theokratie*, 108, n.28). The rubrics have most recently been used by Bunge (*Untersuchungen*, 175-181) in his attempt to uncover the five-volume work of Jason of Cyrene. Jason's work would have been structured, according to Bunge, on the reigns of the Seleucid kings. Bunge holds that the rubric at 2 Macc 7:42 was added because of the length of the material on Antiochus IV. That the rubric at 3:40 does not coincide with a dynastic change does not worry him, for the work of the author was not of an historical but of an edifying nature. Therefore the author divides his work not by reigns, but by the defense of the temple. Bunge's use of the rubrics falls with his source-critical theories. One could also point out that the rubric at 2 Macc 15:37 surely shows that the author of the work was at home with the phraseology. One should therefore treat these rubrics as indicators of the narrative of the epitome, not as leftovers from the work of Jason.

[83] This theme of the book may explain why the author speaks of the Seleucid forces as "barbarians" at 2 Macc 2:21. Such a reversal of normal Greek usage would point to the Jews as the cultured race, part of Greek society, not those who attack them.

CHAPTER FOUR

THE LITERARY CHARACTER OF 2 MACCABEES*

The writer of the narrative in 2 Maccabees clearly states that his work is an "epitome" of a larger history of the period by a Jason of Cyrene. Throughout the prologue to his work, the author insists on the contrast "long-short." As the meaning of some of these contrasts has sometimes been obscured, they repay a closer look.

2:24: *to chyma tōn arithmōn*: This phrase has been translated in all kinds of ways and used frequently to denigrate the work of the author. A few examples of such translations are: "the flood of statistics" (Goodspeed); "le flot des chiffres" (Abel); "den Schwall von Zahlen" (Habicht). If the phrase is translated in this way, the author is presumed to disdain facts and figures and to show that he himself is not at all an historian. For Abel, the phrase means that the author is going to avoid the dullness of a chronicle, and choose interesting events to write about in a literary manner.[1] But this is not at all the case. *To chyma tōn arithmōn* may simply mean that Jason's work has a great number of pages. The phrase in the same verse, *to plēthos tēs hylēs* "the abundance of subject matter,"—which, while not linguistically parallel, is parallel in thought—implies a long treatment, as does the fact that Jason wrote five books about the subject. Now the length of books was counted in terms of written lines, called *stichoi*; the total number of *stichoi* per book, or papyrus roll, was given at the end of the copy as a comprehensive number. In the Herculanean papyri of the 1st cent. B.C.E., the term *arithmos* is used in giving this number of lines.[2] In the work of the 1st cent. author on medicine, Apollonius of Citium, *arithmos* is equivalent to *stichos*.

---

* A condensed version of my treatment of "tragic" history and 2 Maccabees first appeared in "2 Maccabees and 'Tragic History'" *HUCA* 50 (1979) 107-114, and there is some overlap in word choice.

[1] Abel, ad 2:24: "Il évitera la sécheresse d'une chronique en faisant un choix de faits intéressants qu'il présentera avec tous les agréments d'une narration littéraire." W.H. Brownlee: the author of the epitome "describes his process as one of omitting tedious and uninteresting matters and of embellishing the material appropriated in order to improve its literary style" (art. "Maccabees, Books of," *IDB* 3.207).

[2] See K. Ohly, "Die Stichometrie der Herkulanischen Rollen," *Archiv für Papyrusforschung* 7 (1924) 190-220; K. Ohly, *Stichometrische Untersuchungen* (Beiheft zum Zentralblatt für Bibliothekswesen 61; Leipzig: Harrassowitz, 1928).

Apollonius is drawing together and illustrating, for a friend, Hippocrates'
Peri Arthrōn. After quoting Hippocrates (cited by the editor as 4.130 L), he
then says: *meta pleionas de arithmous outōs phēsin*, and then quotes
4.134 L. The word *arithmous* must be translated to mean "lines of a book,"
i.e., "after many lines, he says . . . "[3] *Arithmos* is found with this meaning
many times in Apollonius in the phrase *meta tinas arithmous*, "after a few
lines."[4] As for *chyma*, there is evidence in the papyri that it was used to
denote a quantitative measure. The evidence comes from a papyrus dated
265 C.E., but it is a legal contract concerning the sale of wine, and so would
have used stereotyped language rather than unusual language.

> (from the property) called Abok near the village Chusis in light new
> wine—jars from unadulterated sweet new wine, in an amount by which
> the whole produce will be drawn off there (*en chymati hō to holon
> genēma exantleitai enthade*) at the time of the vintage in Oxyrhynchos.
> On each trip from the property to the metropolis, half (of the amount)
> will be transported.[5]

In a similar document from the same vineyard in the same year, the contract
has instead of *en chymati hō to holon genēma* the phrase *metrō hō to holon
genēma*.[6] Thus, *chyma* is equivalent to *metron* in these texts.

So in 2 Maccabees, *chyma* would also have the meaning of "quantity"
or "amount," not "confused mass" or "flood," and implies something
between an exact measure and a large quantity.[7] The phrase, *to chyma tōn
arithmōn*, which is clearly metaphorical, would thus have a meaning
approaching "a large number of lines," a meaning which would fit the context perfectly. The author, seeing how people were put off from reading
historical accounts because they are too long, i.e., have too many lines and
too much subject matter, has undertaken to solve this problem by publishing
a shortened version of one of these long tomes. By so doing, he aims at
providing *psychagōgia* to those who wish to read, ease for those who strive
to memorize, and usefulness for everyone.[8] This sentence sets forth the program of the author, and therefore needs to be treated in some detail.

---

[3]   Apollonius Citiensis, ed. H. Schöne (Leipzig: Teubner, 1896) 11.8.
[4]   9.6; 13.14; 18.26; 19.9; 30.5. E. Bickerman had pointed to this meaning in "Notes in
the Greek Book of Esther," *Studies in Jewish and Christian History. Part 1.* (Arbeiten zur
Geschichte des antiken Judentums und des Urchristentums 9; Leiden: Brill, 1976) 256, n. 36.
[5]   *Papiri greci e latini XII* (Pubblicazioni della Società Italiana per la ricerca dei Papiri
greci e latini in Egitto; ed. M. Norsa; Firenze; E. Ariani, 1943) no. 1250.
[6]   No. 1249. 26-27.
[7]   In a private communication, E. G. Turner suggested the word "tankful."
[8]   I have accepted the emendation proposed by B. Risberg ("Textkritische und exege-
tische Anmerkungen zu den Makkabäerbuchern," *Beiträge zur Religionswissenschaft hrsg. von*

What the author is furnishing is *psychagōgia*, ease (*eukopia*) in recollecting from memory, and utility (*ōpheleia*). These are conventional commonplaces of Hellenistic historiography. This is particularly so of the pair pleasure and profit. That history should be both pleasurable and useful was a rhetorical topos, found in authors like Polybius, Cicero, Diodorus Siculus, Dionysius of Halicarnassus, Josephus, Lucian, and Cassius Dio.[9] Isocrates earlier had distinguished between discourses which gave useful advice and teaching and those which abounded in crowd-tickling stories of contests and battles and games among the demi-gods (*Ad Nicoclem* 48-49). Thucydides applied this same distinction to history when, in his programmatic statement about the task of the historian, he wrote: "And it may be that the absence of the fabulous from my narrative will seem less pleasing to the ear; but whoever shall wish to have a clear view, both of the events which happened, and of those which some day, in all human probability, happen again in the same or a similar way—for these to adjudge my history profitable will be enough for me" (1.22.4). Polybius followed this lead in preferring utility to pleasure, and this preference itself became commonplace.[10] The author of the epitome is going to give his readers pleasure by writing a short history. By the brevity of his work, he will silence the complaints of those who find the abundance of material in histories tiresome, but his work will also be useful. In phrasing his aims, he uses the standard terminology of Hellenistic historians.

The author also furnishes his short work as an aide-mémoire.[11] Other Hellenistic historians were conscious of the need to help the memory. Diodorus Siculus, in his introduction to Bk 16, wrote: "In all systematic historical treatises, it behooves the historian to include in his books actions of states or of kings which are complete in themselves from beginning to end; for so I conceive history to become most easy to remember and most intelligible to the reader (*eumnēmoneuton kai saphē genesthai*)." While other

---

der *religionswissenschaftlichen Gesellschaft in Stockholm* [Stockholm/Leipzig: A. Bonnier/ J.C. Hinrich, 1918] 2.18-19) and accepted by P. Katz ("The Text," 13) and C. Habicht, that φιλοπονοῦσιν be read instead of φιλοφρονοῦσιν. The active φιλοφρονέω would be very unusual in this sense (usually the middle has this meaning), and φιλοπονέω fits the context admirably. Hanhart disagrees ("Zum Text," 460).

[9] Plb 15.36.3; 1.4.11; 6.1.3 and 8; *1.1.8*; 32.16.1; 39.19.7; Cicero *Fin* 5.19.51; D. S. 1.3.5; 20.2.1; D. H. 1.1.2; 5.56.1; *Pomp* 6; Jos *Ant* 14.2-3; Lucian *Hist. Conscr.* 13; 39; 42; 61; 63; Cassius Dio 1.1.4. See P. Scheller, *De hellenistica historiae conscribendae arte* (Leipzig: R. Noshe, 1911) 72-78.

[10] Plb 2.56.11; 3.31.13; 12.25b.2; 38.6.8.

[11] Of course, brevity is by itself an aid to memory. See the link between memorization and the epitomes which Epicurus (Diogenes Laertius 10.35-38; 10.84 and 116) and Plutarch (*Coniugalia Praecepta* 138C) drew up. In the following, I have brought into play the role of memory in the construction of histories.

authors do not explicitly speak of memory, their attention to making their
account a unit might be allied to it. Cicero thought that his part in the
Roman civil wars would make a nice monograph, since it would center
around one person and one self-contained event.[12] Polybius, too, insists that
his universal history has, after all, only one theme: how Fortune guided all
the affairs of the world in one direction and forced them to incline towards
one and the same end, the dominion of Rome (1.4.1).[13] As Aristotle said of
tragedy, well constructed plots must not begin and end at random. "As then
creatures and other organic structures must have a certain magnitude and
yet be easily taken in by the eye (*eusynopton*), so too with plots: they must
have a length but must be easily taken in by the memory (*eumnēmoneuton*)."[14] The author of the epitome is helping his readers by not burying their
memories in too much detail.

At 2 Macc 2:26-27, the author tells how he has undertaken this labor for
the benefit of others willingly—another rhetorical cliché.[15]

He continues his contrast "long-short" with a series of phrases in vv 28-
31, which set off the work of authors of complete histories from that of
authors of epitomes.

Complete Histories	*Epitomes*
a minute presentation of details	passing in review the events by means of the main points
the author is like the architect of a complete building	the author of an epitome is like a painter and decorator
enter into a subject and discuss it so that every detail is thoroughly investigated	treat of a subject briefly,[16] and avoid complete treatment

---

[12] Cicero, *Epis.Fam.* 5.12. For a full discussion of this idea, see G. Avenarius, *Lukians
Schrift zur Geschichtsschreibung* (Meisenheim/Glan: Hain, 1956) 105-113.

[13] Cf. also Plb 3.1.4-5 and 9. At 1.3.4, Polybius speaks of his work as a body. As F. W.
Walbank notes: "The concept of such a πραγματεία as a σῶμα reaches Polybius from Hellenis-
tic historiography; cf. Dion.Hal. *ad Pomp.* 3; *Thuc.* 5f.; 10; *Diod.* XX,1.5. . . . The idea derives
ultimately from the Platonic Aristotelian concept of the unity of a literary work: cf. Plato
Phaedr. 264c; Aris. *Poetics* 24,1. 1459a17f" (*A Historical Commentary on Polybius* [Oxford:
Oxford Univ., 1957] 1.43).

[14] Aristotle *Poetics* 7.10 (1451a). Aristotle, of course, did not think that such a theory of
tragedy applied to history (*Poetics* 23.1). However, G. Giovannini has gathered numerous
examples to show that Aristotle's position on this subject in antiquity was the "heretical" one.
("The Connection between Tragedy and History in Ancient Criticism," *Philological Quarterly* 22 [1943] 308-314.)

[15] Cf. D.S. 1.3.6; 1.4.1, where the same terminology as in 2 Maccabees is found.

[16] *To syntomon tēs lexeōs* "brevity of speech." The contrasted v 30 and the parallel in v

The contrast painter-architect ought not to lead one astray: the author is not using the image to state that he is polishing up the work of Jason or that he is adding to it the ornaments of a good style.[17] Lucian does compare the way the historian works to that of a sculptor who fashions and reshapes the material of his craft—a bare record of events is not enough: events have to be arranged properly, and the whole written in as fine a style as possible.[18] The author of the epitome is not contrasting bare walls with painted ones: he is contrasting two crafts—one which deals with the whole project, and one which is more specialized. He is contrasting a full exposition of the facts versus a selective presentation.

In the whole prologue, then, the author is concerned with size, with contrasting the burdensome length of Jason's work with his own short compass. No conclusions should be drawn about the qualities of the respective works, either that Jason's was dull or a chronicle of events, or that the epitome is a rhetorical exercise with no concern for history. To draw such conclusions would be to miss the point of the prologue and to misinterpret.

The author is thus shortening, or epitomizing, a larger work. From this two questions arise: 1) Did, in fact, such a larger work exist? 2) If so, can one say anything about the relation of the larger work to the shorter?

As to the first question, W. Richnow has recently argued that Jason is a literary fiction.[19] He argues from the term "epitome," from the fact that five books is not really that long, and from the fact that Jason's name never appears again in the work while, on the contrary, the author emphatically ends his work with "I will cease" with no reference to Jason. Finally, Richnow notes that the practice of inventing authors to give authority to one's own work was widespread in antiquity. For Richnow, the epitome in 2 Maccabees is another instance of such a practice.

Richnow does not discuss the problems against such a theory: the introduction by the author of events and persons for whom there has been no preparation as, for example, the people and episodes at 8:30-33. Besides this, however, Richnow's thesis does not hold. He does not seem to have consulted the lists of what were considered to be epitomes in antiquity. One of the earliest historians to whom an epitome is ascribed, Theopompus of Chios, is said to have epitomized the nine books of Herodotus into two, i.e., the same proportion almost as that of 2 Maccabees. In fact, the customary proportion is from a third to a fifth of the original. A certain Menippus, who

---

31b show that there is no question here of a stylistic virtue, as in *ad Herennium* 4.68; Demetr. *De eloc.* 137, but simply of a short text.

[17] See footnote 1.

[18] Lucian *Hist. Conscr.* 16; 50-51.

[19] W. Richnow, "Untersuchungen," 41-42.

is dated before 100 B.C.E., wrote an epitome of the four books on Lydian history by Xanthus.[20] Secondly, one does not see why the name of Jason should appear again in the work. In the epilogue, the author is saying that his work has come to an appropriate end. As for the practice in antiquity of inventing authors, when one examines the evidence one finds no case where reference is made to a non-existent book concerned with *recent* historical events. The authors referred to as stating that non-existent books were used as references are Seneca, Pliny, Quintilian, and Lucian.[21] But the statement of Pliny on the lies told and accepted by Greeks comes in the context of discussing tales of how men change to wolves and back again (*HN* 8.82). Seneca (*QN* 4.3.1; 7.16) attacks historians who explain physical phenomena incorrectly; e.g., Ephorus said that a comet split into two comets when Helice and Buris were destroyed by earthquake. Such a statement is incredible to Seneca because, in his theory, comets are not made of the same material as planets. Quintilian holds that abuses occur chiefly in fabulous stories when authors, writing about what is far off or never existed, can invent whole books and authors, "whereas if the subject is familiar the careful investigator will often detect the fraud" (*Inst* 1.8.21). Lucian speaks of inventing authors in the context of academic one-upmanship (*Rh. Pr.* 17).

Ptolemaeus Chennos is said to be the example of a writer who invents authorities out of thin air for whatever he says. But when one examines the extract of the work in Photius,[22] one finds that the invented authors are said to be the precursors of Homer and that those authors of whom we know nothing more than the names are talking of the remote heroic past, particularly the life of Heracles. As for the precursors of Homer, these reflect polemical traditions: Helen, daughter of the Athenian Mousaios, or the girl from Memphis, Phantasia, whose copy Homer took when he passed by there. Rationalistic, as well as nationalistic, traditions are at play here. The same may be said of Strabo, 1.2.9, where Strabo places Homer and historians together in that they both make use of myths and tales of far-off places to amuse and hold the attention of their audience.[23] Another alleged case of

---

[20] FGH 115 T 1. FGH 766 (= Diogenes Laertius 6.101).

[21] For a full discussion, see H. Peter, *Wahrheit und Kunst, Geschichtsschreibung und Plagiat im classischen Altertum* (Leipzig/ Berlin: Teubner, 1911); E. Stemplinger, *Das Plagiat in der griechischen Literatur* (Leipzig/ Berlin: Teubner, 1912); W. Speyer, *Die literarische Fälschung im heidnischen und christlichen Altertum; ein Versuch ihrer Deutung* (Munich: Beck, 1971). Speyer, although he has a section on Jewish writings, does not mention 2 Maccabees.

[22] Edited by A. Chatzis, *Der Philosoph und Grammatiker Ptolemaios Chennos* (Paderborn: F. Schöningh, 1914).

[23] D.H. *ad Pomp.* 6 links *psychagōgia* and *ōphelia* by holding that narratives about the establishment of cities, the foundation of nations, the portrayal of lives and kings and peculiar customs are both entertaining and useful, and belong to the realm of history.

inventing works is that of Xenophon's referral to Themistogenes the Syracusan in *Hellenica* 3.1.2, which Plutarch saw as covering up his own authorship of the *Anabasis* (Plu *On the Fame of the Athenians* 345e). But this is not a question of inventing a book, but a name.

As can be seen, false authorities are made up for events which fell in the mythical past, for descriptions of far-off places, and for exceedingly unusual natural phenomena , which also usually occur in remote areas inaccessible to the average reader. There are no instances where books relating to recent events are invented.

Finally, note must be taken of the different types of epitome. The term, which had first been applied to the shortened version of the work of one author, began to be used for a short treatment of some subject matter. An epitome of genealogies is ascribed to Andron of Halicarnassus, an author of the 4th cent. B.C.E.[24] Phylarchus is said to have written an epitome of mythologies.[25] As I. Opelt remarks, *epitomae rei tractatae* are much more numerous than *epitomae auctoris* in the late Roman period.[26] When Richnow thus holds that the epitome of 2 Maccabees is like that of Plutarch's *Life of Alexander*, he is comparing apples and oranges. For Plutarch simply states that he is going to epitomize the most celebrated parts of the lives of Alexander and Caesar rather than deal with every particular episode in detail. Plutarch is writing an *epitoma rei tractatae*, not an *epitoma auctoris*, and he cannot be used in a comparison to hold that Jason of Cyrene is a literary fiction.[27]

In conclusion, the arguments of Richnow to show that Jason of Cyrene is a literary fiction are not convincing. One has to take the author of 2 Maccabees at face value when he claims that he is writing an epitome of a larger work, of which, unfortunately, no copy exists.

If the work of Jason of Cyrene is lacking, can one gain knowledge of it from the epitome? Unfortunately, the author in his prologue has not taken any stance vis-à-vis Jason. Justin had said that he had left out from his epitome of Pompeius Trogus everything that was not desirable to know or necessary as examples.[28] Marcian of Heraclea of Pontus was quite explicit in stating that he had added to the authors he was epitomizing whatever was missing from their work: "I have made clear what is an epitome of their labors and what are my own corrections, so that whoever reads the work will

---

[24] FGH 10 F 5.

[25] FGH 81 T 1.

[26] I. Opelt, art. "Epitome," *RAC* 5.945.

[27] W. Richnow, "Untersuchungen," 42.

[28] *M. Iuliani Iustini Epitoma historiarum philippicarum Pompei Trogi*, ed. M. Galdi (Turin: G. B. Paravia, 1927).

not be ignorant of what was written by them, and what has been added by me or what I have considered a better correction. "[29] Our author has not done this and, as has been shown above, he has left no clues as to how he handled the work of Jason, besides shortening the text. Since source-criticism is of no avail in distinguishing the work of Jason of Cyrene from the epitome, one must remain content with studying the epitome itself. However, epitome is not a sufficiently specific literary-critical term. One must look further to establish the literary character of 2 Maccabees.

The Author and Tragic History

In the prologue to the narrative, the author contrasts what he is doing with the work of historians. His is a selective process, whereas they treat a matter completely. While his work is contrasted with theirs, then, it is also bound to them. The epitome, too, is history.

But what kind of history? Since the original study of B. Niese in 1900, commentators have answered: tragic history, the predominant genre of Hellenistic historiography. Niese, in fact, used the term "rhetorical" historiography, Bickermann spoke of "pathetic" historiography, while Habicht combined the two and talked of "pathetic and rhetorical" historiography.[30] All these writers, however, are envisaging a definite *Gattung* of historiography which is "tragic" history. In his discussion, Niese gave as examples of such a genre the works of Theopompus, Cleitarchus, and Phylarchus.[31] However, at almost the same time as Niese was writing, E. Schwartz was distinguishing even further the field of Hellenistic historiography.[32] Theopompus would belong to a school of historiography conforming to the stylistic demands of Isocrates; Cleitarchus to a revived Ionic style of history writing; and Phylarchus to a type originating with the Peripatetics.[33] Since the pioneering work of Schwartz, discussion proceeded, with each author attempting to find out who discovered "tragic" history writing. E. Will sought to see in Callisthenes the first representative of tragic history;

---

[29] From the edition of C. Müller, *Geographi Graeci Minores* (Hildesheim: G. Olms, 1965—reproduction of the edition Paris: Firmin-Didot, 1882) 1.567.19-33. Marcian is epitomizing the works of Artemidorus of Ephesus, geographer, and Menippus of Pergamum.

[30] B. Niese, *Kritik*, 33-34; E. Bickermann, *Der Gott der Makkabäer. Untersuchungen über Sinn und Ursprung der makkabäischen Erhebung* (Berlin: Schocken, 1937) 147; C. Habicht, 189. Also, A. Momigliano, "Greek Historiography," *History and Theory* 17 (1978) 8.

[31] B. Niese, *Kritik*, 33-34.

[32] E. Schwartz, *Fünf Vorträge über den griechischen Roman* (Berlin: G. Reimer, 1896; I have used the second edition: Berlin: de Gruyter, 1943).

[33] In particular, see E. Schwartz, "Berichte über die catilinarische Verschwörung," *Hermes* 32 (1897) 560.

F. Wehrli derived it from Gorgias.[34] B. L. Ullman tried to show that the main Hellenistic historians derived their techniques from Isocrates.[35] K. von Fritz suggested Aristotle,[36] and N. Zegers followed this suggestion when he tried to show that Duris and Phylarchus followed in their histories Aristotle's rules for tragedy.[37] Duris, in fact, was often seen as the originator of a new type of history writing as he adapted Aristotle's rules for rhetoric to history. Criticising Theopompus and Ephorus, Duris said that their writings lacked *mimēsis* and *hēdonē* (FGH 76 F1). These terms, frequently found in Aristotle's *Poetics*, were thought to herald a programmatic tragedization of history. However, K. Meister's analysis of these terms in their context shows that this is not the case. For Duris, *mimēsis* means imitation of what happened—*mimēsis tōn genomenōn*—not a theatrical interpretation of reality.[38] This interpretation of Meister's agrees completely with R. Kebric's view of Duris:

> Perhaps the most significant evidence to lay to rest the idea that he lighted upon "tragic history" as a result of a particular literary theory can be found in Duris' own use of sources. Beginning with Herodotus, it seems he deliberately sought out compatible sources which contained elements of the "tragic," whether they be Peripatetics, Isocrateans or other. This is indicated even among the pitiful remains of his *History*. The most sensible conclusion, then, is that Duris was conscious of his own debt to these earlier historians and considered himself the continuator of an old tradition—not the founder of a new one.[39]

The more authors have sought to find a definite originator of "tragic" history, the clearer it has become that the connection between tragedy and

---

[34] E. Will, *Kallisthenes' Hellenika* (Königsberg: Hartung, 1913) 76; F. Wehrli, "Die Geschichtsschreibung im Lichte der antiken Theorie," *Eumusia. Festgabe für E. Howald* (Erlenbach-Zurich: Rentsch, 1947) 54-71.

[35] B. L. Ullman, "History and Tragedy," *TAPA* 73 (1942) 25-53.

[36] K. von Fritz, "Die Bedeutung des Aristotles für die Geschichtsschreibung," *Histoire et Historiens dans l'Antiquité* (Fondation Hardt, Entretiens 4: Vandoeuvres-Genève, 1956) 85-128. Also, *Aristotle's Contribution to the theory and practice of historiography* (Berkeley: U. of California Press, 1958).

[37] N. Zegers, *Wesen und Ursprung der tragischen Geschichtsschreibung* (Cologne: Universität zu Köln, 1959). Also, H. Strasburger, *Die Wesensbestimmung der Geschichte durch die antike Geschichtsschreibung* (Wiesbaden: F. Steiner, 1966).

[38] K. Meister, *Historische Kritik bei Polybios* (Palingenesia 9; Wiesbaden: F. Steiner, 1975) 113-115. As for *hēdonē*, Meister writes: "Gemeint ist die Freude, die man an einer wirklichkeitsgetreuen Darstellung empfindet. Ist es doch eine Erfahrungstatsache, daß eine derartige Schilderung den Leser packt und fesselt" (115).

[39] R. B. Kebric, *In the Shadow of Macedon: Duris of Samos* (Historia Einzelschriften 29; Wiesbaden: F. Steiner, 1977) 18.

history was longstanding and deep. The work of M. Laistner showed that the two art forms were linked in the 5th cent. B.C.E.,[40] and Giovannini has shown that Aristotle's separation of history and tragedy in the *Poetics* (23.1) was the aberration, not the norm.[41] Ctesias (late 5th cent. B.C.E.) enjoyed developing the dramatic potential of historical situations: Demetrius testifies that by the description in Ctesias of how the news of Cyrus' death was gradually announced to Queen Parysatis the reader becomes involved in the grief of the queen.[42] Herodotus enjoyed a good story, and even Thucydides evoked emotion in his readers. "Sometimes Thucydides makes the sufferings so cruel, so terrible, and so deserving of pity that he leaves nothing worse for either historians or poets to describe" (*D.H. de Thuc* 15). Plutarch says that Thucydides makes his hearers spectators of the events (Plu *de glor Athen* 347a). Walbank summed up the conclusions of earlier studies when he wrote:

> There existed in reality a long-standing affinity between the two art-forms of history and tragedy, based on a common subject matter in the panhellenic legends (which were universally regarded as true), on the fact that both made their appeal to easily aroused emotions—for history like poetry was normally read aloud, on a common emphasis on moral purpose shared by both, and on an identical background in the schools of rhetoric, which exploited both historical and tragic *exempla* for their own ends.[43]

Walbank would like to discard the term "tragic history" from future discussion, as "the sharp isolation of 'tragic history' as a separate school in need of explanation and of a definite and immediate ancestry is very largely a figment and a distortion."[44] Tragic history "is a far less homogeneous literary form—whether in Greece or followed through in Latin literature—than some discussion of it has suggested."[45] This lack of homogeneity is further underlined when one considers that Polybius, the most antitragic of all, wrote emotionally and tragically. Clear examples of this are found in Polybius' description of the fall of Agathocles in 15.24-33, where the growing hatred of the populace towards Agathocles is vividly pictured as are the deaths of Agathocles' followers, and 16.30-34, the siege of Abydus, during which the besieged all killed themselves rather than fall into Philip V's

---

[40] M. Laistner, *The Greater Roman Historians* (Sather Classical Lectures 21; Berkeley: U. of California Press, 1947) 12-13.

[41] G. Giovannini, "The Connection," 308-314.

[42] Demetrius *de Eloc.* 215-216.

[43] F. W. Walbank, *Polybius* (Berkeley: U. of California Press, 1972) 38.

[44] F. W. Walbank, "History and Tragedy," *Historia* 9 (1960) 233-234.

[45] F. W. Walbank, "Tragic History," *Bulletin of the Institute of Classical Studies of the University of London* 2 (1955) 12.

hands. Even more tragic is the account of the last years of Philip V, which will be discussed below. These examples from Polybius underline the fact that there is no such defined genre as "tragic history."

One should not forget, in fact, that the term "tragic history" derives from polemic. "'Tragic' is no more than a label selected by Polybius to vilify a school of historians, whose faults were approximately those of our contemporary press."[46] One sees the same trace of polemic in Cicero when he speaks of authors describing the death of Themistocles:

> As you like, since the privilege is conceded to rhetoricians to distort history in order to give more point to their narrative. Like your story of Coriolanus' death, Clitarchus and Stratocles both have invented an account of the death of Themistocles. But Thucydides, a native Athenian of high birth and distinction, and only a little later in time, merely says that he died a natural death and was buried secretly in Attic soil, adding that rumor said he had taken his own life by poison. The others say that on sacrificing a bullock, he drank a bowl of its blood and from that draught fell dead. This is a kind of death that gave them the chance for rhetorical and tragic treatment; the ordinary natural death gave them no such opportunity.[47]

It is the same Cicero, however, who has given what is perhaps the fullest disquisition on how to dramatize history: he feels that his life is "a drama rich in acts and scenes"; his part in the Roman civil wars would make a nice monograph, which would center around one person and one self-contained event.[48] Cicero would not even mind if Lucceius were a trifle enthusiastic in his coloring of Cicero's actions.[49] Again, Plutarch rails against Phylarchus as being dramatic: "Everybody knows that Phylarchus makes up things in his *Histories* where he practically drags in stage machinery and introduces Neocles and Demopolis as the sons of Themistocles to arouse sympathy, just like a tragedian." However, Plutarch leans heavily on that same Phylarchus for his life of Cleomenes and prefers him in places to Polybius.[50] This is especially so in the account of the death of Cleomenes, where Polybius may be

---

[46] F. W. Walbank, "ΦΙΛΙΠΠΟΣ ΤΡΑΓΩΙΔΟΥΜΕΝΟΣ: A Polybian Experiment," *JHS* 58 (1938) 58.

[47] *Brutus* 43.

[48] Cicero, *Epis.Fam.* 5.12.

[49] Cicero, *Epis.Fam.* 5.12.3.

[50] T. W. Africa, *Phylarchus and the Spartan Revolution* (Berkeley: U. of California Press, 1961) 40-41. E. Gabba ("Studi su Filarco. Le biografie plutarchee di Agide e di Cleomene [Capp. I-IV]," *Athenaeum* 35 [1957] 220-226) has given an excellent description of Phylarchus' attempts to draw in and involve his readers, and of the reasons why Plutarch chose Phylarchus over Polybius.

too tragic: Phylarchus attributes treachery of Nicagoras to a debt owed, Polybius to the fact that Nicagoras had been innocently involved in the treacherous death of Archidamus.[51] To call a work "tragic," then, is simply to relegate it to the second rank.

In what does Polybius' polemical use of "tragic history" consist? In Book 2, Polybius is particularly disparaging of Phylarchus for his striving after emotional effect. Phylarchus is

> always trying to bring horrors vividly before our eyes. . . . A historical author should not try to thrill his readers by such exaggerated pictures, nor should he, like a tragic poet, try to imagine the probable utterances of his characters or reckon up all the consequences probably incidental to the occurrences with which he deals, but simply record what really happened and what really was said, however commonplace. . . . Apart from this, Phylarchus simply narrates most of such catastrophes and does not even suggest their causes, without which it is impossible in any case to feel either legitimate pity or proper anger (2.56.8-14).

The issue of sensational writing is bound up with the issue of causes. Phylarchus, according to Polybius, insisted on the cruelty of Antigonus and the Macedonians and also Aratus and the Achaeans, but did not properly point out the reason for this: the Mantineans had revolted from the Achaean cause and had massacred the garrison of Achaeans whom the Mantineans had earlier requested for defense. Polybius of course does not mention that, to gain support in Mantinea, Aratus gave citizenship to metics and introduced Achaean settlers into the city. Nor does he mention that Aratus, by calling in the Macedonians, betrayed Achaia. In short, Phylarchus is bad according to Polybius because he is pro-Spartan. Polybius is violently against Sparta and, in particular, Cleomenes who had razed Polybius' birthplace, Megalopolis. The emotional description by Phylarchus of the captives at Mantinea is wrong and bad history writing, because the Mantineans were rebels against the Achaean cause and deserved all they got. For Polybius, Phylarchus' description is vitiated by the wrong premise of the goodness of Cleomenes, king of Sparta: thus, his whole history is wrong.

> The fall of Megalopolis, the execution of Aristomachus, and the sack of Mantinea all touched raw nerves of Achaean guilt, while the issue of collaboration with Cleomenes raised a family ghost which could be exorcised only by attacking the man who had called it by name. Far

---

[51] T. W. Africa, *Phylarchus*, 31.

from being scientific, Polybius' famed critique of Phylarchus is simply obscurantist.[52]

An Example of Dramatic Presentation

A fine example of a dramatic treatment of an historical event is provided by Polybius in his account of the last years of Philip V of Macedon.[53] The account is found in the excerpted version of Valesius and Mai, and in Livy, an account which closely follows Polybius.[54] F. W. Walbank, in a masterly article on this subject, has reconstructed the original from Livy:

> This year witnessed the outbreak of disaster for Philip and for Macedon, an event worthy of attention and careful record. Fortune, wishing to punish Philip for all his wicked acts, sent against him a host of furies, torments and avenging spirits of his victims; these tortured him up to the day of his death, never leaving him, so that all realised that, as the proverb goes, "Justice has an eye" and men must not scorn her. [Next come the details of how these furies work—by inspiring infatuation, which leads their victim to commit acts leading to his own downfall.] First these furies inspired Philip to carry out exchanges of population between Thrace and the coast towns, in preparation for his war with Rome; and as a result *men's hatred grew greater than their fear* and they cursed Philip openly. *Eventually, his mind rendered fiercer by these curses, Philip came to feel himself in danger unless he imprisoned the children of those he had killed.* So he wrote to the officers in the various cities and had this done; he had in mind chiefly the children of Admetus, Pyrrhichus and Samus and the rest he had executed at the same time, but he included all who had been put to death by royal command, quoting the line νήπιος ὅς πατέρα κτείνας υἱοὺς καταλείπει. The general effect of this was to awaken pity for the children of men of high station; *but a particular incident brought the corresponding loathing of Philip to a climax. This was the death of Theoxena and her sister's children.* [Here occurred the account of this, as given in Livy.] *This incident added new flame to the hatred of his people, and they now openly cursed Philip and his sons; and these curses, heard by all the gods, caused Philip to turn his anger against his own blood.* For while his mind was almost maddened on this account,

---

[52] T. W. Africa, *Phylarchus*, 33.

[53] Plb 23.10-11.

[54] F. W. Walbank, "A Polybian Experiment," 61. For a discussion of the manuscript tradition, see J. M. Moore, *The Manuscript Tradition of Polybius* (Cambridge: Cambridge Univ. Press, 1965) 130-133.

the quarrel of his sons burst into flame simultaneously, Fortune as if of set purpose bringing their misfortunes on the stage at one and the same time. The quarrel was referred to Philip and he had to decide which of his two sons he should murder and which he should fear as his own possible murderer for the rest of his life. Who can help thinking that the wrath of heaven was descending on him for his past sins? The details that follow will make this clearer. [Then come the details of the quarrel between Demetrius and Perseus: Livy XL,5-24; Pol. XXIII,10,17; 11.][55]

This is basically the introduction of Polybius to Philip's last years. As Walbank has shown, there is a clearly defined sequence of cause and effect in operation. Philip was mistaken, according to Polybius, in planning war on Rome. To prepare for this, he carried out exchanges of population. People were antagonized and, in reprisal, Philip adopted severe measures which were excessive. This excess brought curses on Philip's head. All this occurred when the dispute between Philip's sons was at its height, and the outcome of that quarrel, Philip's killing of his own son, was seen as the answer to the curses. Tyche, Fortune, is the force which connects all these events into one plan of retribution.[56] It is Polybius' concern with moral motivation which has led him to depict Philip's last years in this light: a king, who when young, had been so full of promise ends his years in bitterness because of his evil deeds.

Such a schema of cause and effect is also discernible in 2 Maccabees.

1) The character of Antiochus IV in the early section of the work is ambivalent: he treats the high-priesthood like any other cultic priesthood, allowing it to be bought and sold, and he is persuaded to give an unjust decision on the advice of a friend; however, he is outraged at the treacherous murder of Onias by Andronicus (4:36-38).[57] The misfortunes of Antiochus begin when he overreacts to reports coming to him about Jerusalem. He thinks that Judea is in revolt (5:11) and so he enacts harsh and excessive measures against the city; he also despoils the temple. This excess brings down on Antiochus' head the prayers of the persecuted (7:14.16-17.18. 19.31.38). These prayers ensure Antiochus' downfall. Antiochus in his excess

---

[55] F. W. Walbank, "A Polybian Experiment," 61-62.

[56] F. W. Walbank, "A Polybian Experiment," 62-63.

[57] I disagree with Richnow ("Untersuchungen," 149-152) who holds that this righteous anger of Antiochus was ascribed to him simply as a literary foil to the dastardly deeds of Menelaus and Andronicus. Such a view rests on the assumption that the author always portrayed Antiochus IV as evil and any change from that is to be explained away as due to literary demands. This is a very static conception of character to ascribe to the author; he certainly does not think of all non-Jews as bad (2 Macc 4:35.49; 12:29-31). Of course literary factors were involved in this depiction of Antiochus, but that does not mean that one has to explain away his good action to maintain a consistently evil characterization.

had not understood his role as instrument of god's chastisement against Israel for its sins, but had acted arrogantly. His death results from this arrogance, as he himself realizes (9:11-12). The final act is the restoration of the despoiled temple.

(2) In 2 Maccabees 14, Nicanor first acts as an honorable man in his dealings with Judas (14:23-25). When he is commanded to act unjustly against Judas, he regrets the action but obeys the command (14:27-29). Nicanor overreacts in his search for Judas by threatening the temple (14:32-33) and by acting arrogantly (15:1-5). This arrogance brings on his downfall.

Such a schematic presentation allows one to grasp the cause and effect sequence that is present in both the account of the last years of Philip V of Macedon and in 2 Maccabees. In one, Tyche avenges the misdeeds of Philip's youth; in the other, God acts against the arrogance of Antiochus IV and Nicanor. This comparison is heightened if one takes into account the role that striking examples play in both accounts. In the account about Philip V, mention was made of the deaths of Theoxena and her sister's children. This story is present in Livy, and both Walbank and Nissen state that it derives from Polybius.[58] Theoxena, a widow with one child, married her dead sister's husband so that she might bring up the children properly. The decision of Philip to slay descendants of his former victims applied to her and her children. Rather than submit, she and her household set out to flee by ship. However, they were pursued along the shore by the king's men, and bad weather was forcing their boat towards land. Rather than fall into the hands of the king, Theoxena, her husband, and the children committed suicide, some by poison, some by the knife, all by jumping into the sea. It was this horrendous deed that focused the hatred of the people against Philip. One can see how the deaths of Eleazar (2 Macc 6:18-31) and Rhazis (2 Macc 14:37-46) illustrate the depths of the persecution, but it is particularly in the story of the martyrdom of the mother and her seven sons, a martyrdom which changes the anger of God to mercy (7:37-38; 8:5), that one can see a significant structural usage.

Polybius adopts a moralist's stance towards Philip V: Tyche takes revenge on Philip for his early misdeeds. The author of the epitome views the crime as an insult to God:

Not content with this, he dared to go into the most holy temple in all the world . . . and took the sacred plate in his polluted hands, and with his

---

[58] F. W. Walbank, "A Polybian Experiment," 61; H. Nissen, *Kritische Untersuchungen über die Quellen der vierten und fünften Dekade des Livius* (Berlin: Weidmann, 1863) 234. As Walbank states: "the story of Theoxena, reproduced in Livy, is so relevant to its place and so rrelevant to Livy's own subject, that it cannot have come from any source but Polybius."

profane hands he swept away what had been dedicated by other kings to enhance the glory and honor of the place. In the elation of his spirit, Antiochus did not realize that it was because of the sins of the inhabitants of the city that the Lord was angered for a little, so that he did not take care of the place (2 Macc 5:15-17).

Prominent here is the theme of attack on a temple, a theme which was discussed in the previous chapter. Here too Antiochus is seen as an instrument of divine punishment, a view also expressed at 2 Macc 10:4, but an instrument which itself is doomed to divine punishment because of its own hubris. Such a theme is frequent in biblical literature: Isa 10:5-19; 47:6-15; Zech 1:15; and, in a more general warning to Israel's enemies, Deut 32:27-38. The two themes of attack on a temple of Jerusalem and the erring instrument of God are linked in 2 Kgs 19:21-34 (= Isa 37:21-35), a prophecy of Isaiah against the besieging army of the king of Assyria. The ambassadors of the Assyrian king insult Yahweh by deprecating his ability to protect his people—why should Yahweh be any stronger than the gods of other nations which had been subdued by the mighty Assyrian army? In response to this arrogant boast, Isaiah foretells the death of the king, and the retreat of his army:

> Have you not heard that I determined it long ago? I planned from days of old what now I bring to pass, that you should make fortified cities crash into heaps of ruins, while their inhabitants, shorn of strength, are dismayed and confounded . . . I know your sitting down and your going out and coming in, and your raging against me. Because you have raged against me and your arrogance has come to my ears, I will put my hook in your nose and my bit in your mouth, and I will turn you back on the way by which you came.

Nicanor is guilty of this crime of arrogance, as well as Antiochus IV, but the theme of erring divine instrument is not present in the Nicanor episode.

Thus, the dramatic presentation of the last years of Philip V of Macedon is similar to the account in 2 Maccabees. In Polybius, the motivation is couched in terms of Tyche; in 2 Maccabees, the author uses theme well established in Jewish tradition.

What is also of special interest is a comparison between the dramatic examples of persecution in Polybius and 2 Maccabees. As regards the death of Theoxena and her children, this horrendous case so outrages the people that they openly curse Philip, and they see the effect of their curses in the murder by Philip of one of his own sons. As Walbank noted, it is Tyche which connects the curses and the death of the son.[59]

> For it was now that Tyche, as if she meant to punish Philip at one and the same time for all the wicked acts he had committed in his life, sent to haunt him furies. . . . Tyche inspired him with the notion that . . . he ought to deport with their whole families all men who took part in politics. . . . In consequence were heard curses and imprecations against the king uttered no longer in secret but openly. . . . And the third tragedy which Tyche produced at the same time was that concerning his sons (Plb 23.10.1-12).

In 2 Maccabees, it is the God of Israel who hears the prayers of the martyrs and sees their deaths (7:37-38) and hears the cries of those unjustly slain (8:3-4).[60] Their sufferings are the pre-condition for the turning of God's anger to mercy, and the pre-condition for Judas' success.[61] G. Nickelsburg noted that throughout the whole section from 4:1 on, a basic Jewish schema of sin-punishment-repentance-salvation occurs. This schema runs through Deuteronomy 28-39, and Nickelsburg has recognized the outline in the *Assumption of Moses*.[62] This is particularly significant as the *Assumption of Moses*, which purports to be Moses' prediction of future events in the history of Israel, deals in chapters 5,8,9,10 with the persecution of Antiochus IV. Nickelsburg has shown how these chapters follow a definite structure of sin (5), punishment (8), turning point (9), salvation (10)—a structure rooted in the latter part of the book of Deuteronomy.[63] Particularly significant in the *Assumption of Moses* is that the turning point deals with the death of Taxo and his seven sons at the hands of the persecutors. Taxo exhorts his sons saying: "Let us die rather than transgress the commands of the Lord of Lords, the God of our fathers. For if we do this and die, our blood shall be avenged before the Lord" (9:6-7). Immediately following this exhortation comes an apocalyptic hymn telling of the salvation of the Lord.[64] Such a schema is also found in Jubilees 1; 23:16-31, and also in the *Testaments of the Twelve Patriarchs*.[65] 2 Maccabees 7, then, while it focuses the point of

[59] F. W. Walbank, "A Polybian Experiment," 62-63.

[60] Cf. G. Vermes, "The Targumic Versions of Genesis 4,3-16," ALUOS 3 (1961-62) 81-114, for a full discussion of blood crying from the earth.

[61] See the previous chapter.

[62] G. Nickelsburg, *Resurrection, Immortality, and Eternal Life in Intertestamental Judaism* (HTS 26; Cambridge: Harvard Univ. Press, 1972) 93-109.

[63] G. Nickelsburg, *Resurrection*, 44.

[64] For a discussion of the formal relationship of this narrative to that of 2 Maccabees 7, see R. Doran, "The Martyr: A Synoptic View of the Mother and her Seven Children," 189-190.

[65] G. Nickelsburg, *Resurrection*, 46-47; K. Baltzer, *The Covenant Formulary; in Old Testament, Jewish, and Early Christian Writings*, tr. D. E. Green (Philadelphia: Fortress, 1971) 55-161.

persecution as in the case of Theoxena and her children in the narrative of Polybius, finds its rightful place in a traditional Jewish way of reporting history.[66]

Just Deserts:

An examination of the last years of Philip V of Macedon in the narrative of Polybius would not be complete if one left out of view the motif of adequate punishment for a crime committed, or the motif of just deserts. In the account above, one can see how Philip, because he murdered his enemies' sons, is forced by Tyche to murder one of his own sons. This murder of his own son is also part of a larger plan on the part of Tyche. For Tyche punishes both Philip V of Macedon and Antiochus III for their brutal treatment of the boy-king Ptolemy Epiphanes by having them kill their own sons.[67] Also, as they attempted to destroy Egypt, Tyche raised up Rome to destroy them.[68] Fitting the punishment to the crime is clearly expressed by Polybius in his comments on the fall of Regulus: "He who so short a time previously had refused to pity or take pity on those in distress was now, almost immediately afterwards, led captive to implore pity and mercy in order to save his own life" (Plb 1.35.3).

Such a theme was a common topos. Two clear examples are found in Diodorus Siculus and Plutarch.

While the dynast was thus engaged, the Carthaginians sailed into the great harbor of Syracuse with fifty light boats. They were able to do nothing more, but falling upon two merchant ships from Athens, they sank the ships themselves and cut off the hands of the crews. They had clearly treated with cruelty men who had done them no harm at all, and the gods quickly gave them a sign of this; for immediately, when some of the ships were separated from the fleet in the vicinity of Brettia, they were captured by the generals of Agathocles, and those who were taken alive suffered a fate similar to that which they had inflicted upon their captives (D.S. 19.103.4-5).

In Eleusis, Theseus killed Cercyon, the Arcadian in a wrestling match. And going on a little further, in Erineus, he slew Damastes, otherwise called Procrustes, forcing his body to the size of his own bed, as he himself was used to do with all strangers; this he did in imitation of

---

[66] This Deuteronomic view of history is most clearly seen in the early chapters of Judges particularly 2-3.

[67] F. W. Walbank, *Polybius*, 63. Plb 15.20.5-8; 29.27.11-12.

[68] F. W. Walbank, *Polybius*, 63.

Heracles, who always returned upon his assailants the same sort of violence that they offered to him; he sacrificed Busiris, killed Antaeus in wrestling, and Cycnus in single combat, and Termerus by breaking his skull in pieces (whence, they say, comes the proverb of "a Termerian mischief"), for it seems that Termerus killed passengers that he met by running with his head against them. And so also Theseus proceeded in the punishment of evil men who underwent the same violence from him that they had inflicted upon others, justly suffering after the manner of their own injustice (Plu *Theseus* 11).

The topos had a long history in Greek mythology: one has only to think of the family history of Tantalus and his grandson Atreus, or of the punishment which overtook Laius, father of Oedipus, for carrying off the son of his host, Pelops.

2 Maccabees uses this topos frequently: the fate of Jason and Menelaus; the execution of Andronicus on the same spot where he killed Onias; the pains which attack Antiochus IV (9:6); the fate of Nicanor (15:32-25). The topos is present in the Elijah cycle (1 Kgs 21:17-19; 2 Kgs 9:30-37), and in the *Wisdom of Solomon* 11:5.15-16; 18:3, and in Josephus' description of the death of Apion (*AgAp* 2.143-144).[69] Such a theme gives a nice structural balance.

Reflections:

Digressions were part of Herodotus' plan (4.30), Thucydides used them, and they became a traditional feature of Greek historiography. Polybius remarks that many earlier writers used such digressions to entertain their readers with myths and stories (Plb 38.5-6). N. Zegers has pointed out that Duris and Phylarchus also made use of the digression to offer reflections on the career of their hero. Such reflections were placed by these two authors at turning-points in the story, particularly when there was a major change from fortune to misfortune or vice-versa. The reflections thus concentrated on the extraordinary nature of these changes, and so impressed "on the reader the

[69] See R. Hanhart, "Zum Text," 18, n.4. In his essay, "Zur Zeitrechnung des I und II Makkabäerbuches," *BZAW* 88 (1964) 74, n.33, Hanhart attempted to hold that this topos was peculiarly Jewish; he built on the work of I. Heinemann, "Synkrisis oder äussere Analogie in der Weisheit Salomos,'" *ThZ* 5 (1948) 241-251. Heinemann wished to distinguish between an *inner* relationship between objects, i.e., between good and bad people, which was found in Greek literature, as, e.g., Plutarch's *Lives*, and and *extrinsic* or analogous relationship between objects, e.g., 40 days of scouting in the Exodus story leads to 40 days of wandering in the wilderness. For Heinemann, such an extrinsic relationship would be Jewish. As the examples cited show, this type of distinction is not adequate.

working of Tyche."[70] An example is provided in the life of Agathocles, found in Diodorus Siculus but thought by Zegers to derive from Duris.[71] At D.S. 20.30.1 is the reflection:

> One might with reason note the inconsistency of Fortune and the strange manner in which human events turn out contrary to expectation. For Agathocles, who was outstanding in courage and who had a large army fighting in his support, not only was defeated decisively by the barbarians at the Himeras River, but he even lost the strongest and largest part of his army; whereas the garrison troops left behind at Syracuse, with only a small part of those who had previously been defeated, not only got the better of the Carthaginian army that had besieged them, but even captured Hamilcar alive, the most famous of their citizens. And what was most amazing, one hundred and twenty thousand foot-soldiers and five thousand horsemen were defeated in battle by a small number of the enemy who enlisted deception and terrain on their side; so that the saying is true that many are the false alarms of war.

Polybius uses the excursus in a variety of ways, all of which reflect his own didactic purposes.[72]

The author of 2 Maccabees also uses reflections at 4:16-17; 5:17-20; 6:12-17. These reflections are used to instruct the reader. The first reflection points out the theological significance of what the Hellenizing party was doing; the second explains why Antiochus IV was able to act so cruelly towards the Jews without God stepping in to help; in the third, the author gives parenetic instruction to his readers. The theological interpretation of history is not something new in Jewish historiography: the Deuteronomic school, for example, explained the fall of Samaria (2 Kgs 17:7-18) and the defeat and death of Josiah (2 Kgs 23:26-27) as the results of previous sins. The author follows in this theological tradition, but one notes in his reflections a different tone from that of earlier Jewish historians. Whereas the Deuteronomic school remained anonymous, the author thrusts himself forward with his use of the first person at 2 Macc 6:12. In the other reflections also, one feels that the author is using a technique of Greek historiography placing the narrator outside the events and commenting on them as does Duris in the above example. The passages in 2 Maccabees display the tone and manner of Greek rhetoric rather than of Hebrew narrative style. However, such reflections use the teaching of Jewish tradition: Israel has a special

70 N. Zegers, *Wesen und Ursprung*, 47; 50-51.
71 N. Zegers, *Wesen und Ursprung*, 26-27.
72 F. W. Walbank, *Polybius*, 46-47.

relationship with God, but if she breaks it by her sins, she will inevitably be punished.

To sum up, the argument so far is that the term "tragic history" does not signify a specific genre of Hellenistic historiography and was created in part in a polemical atmosphere. However, this argument in no way implies that the events in 2 Maccabees are not dramatically and "tragically" narrated. As noted frequently in the previous chapter, the author uses all the techniques of rhetorical skill to heighten tension and to structure his events dramatically. Also, as did Phylarchus, so too the author of 2 Maccabees tries in every way to involve his readers: note, for example, the homiletic first person plural in 6:12.15.16. Similarities with the dramatic presentation of the last years of Philip V of Macedon by Polybius have also been noted. However, the author motivates his dramatic presentation of history in a way traditional to Jewish thought.

Tales of the Marvellous

Polybius was polemical against historians who did not share his view of events, and called them "tragic." In his denunciation of other historians, Polybius was also calling for new standards in history-writing. Like Thucydides, he wanted history to serve a political and moral purpose, to instruct readers how to behave. He used his excursuses for this didactic purpose and did not use them to delve into stories of wondrous or mythical events. When discussing the geography of the Po valley, he writes:

> The other tales the Greeks tell about this river, I mean touching Phaeton and his fall and the weeping poplar-trees and the black clothing of the inhabitants near the river, . . . and all material of a tragic character and similar to this legend, we will leave aside for the present, detailed polemic against such things not suiting very well the character of my introduction (2.16.13-14).[73]

Polybius says that he will undertake such polemic later on, particularly as Timaeus has shown much ignorance of the district, but this discussion has not survived. Polybius wanted to teach people how to act in all situations, and so he is against too much sensationalism. At the end of his discussion of Agathocles, Polybius rebukes writers who have introduced sensational accounts, because Agathocles was not, in Polybius' eyes, a fit object "inasmuch as Agathocles displayed neither courage in war nor conspicuous ability, nor was he fortunate and exemplary in his management of affairs, nor,

---

[73] For this interpretation of the passage, see F. W. Walbank, *A Historical Commentary*, 181.

finally, had he that acuteness and mischievous address which serve a court-ier's ends" (15.34.3-4). Tales of marvels and extraordinary and sensational events do not serve any purpose beyond entertaining the reader by holding his attention for a while, but they do not instruct because they are not typical (15.36.1-7). No reader can learn from them how he himself should act in similar circumstances. Polybius does not want stories which contain "the marvelous and the monstrous. . . . as well as the trivial, the meretricious and the sentimental—night scenes, detailed descriptions of clothing, love-interest, and the almost human behaviour of animals."[74] Examples of such stories can be seen in the extant fragments of Duris and Phylarchus. Duris has stories about the love of a dolphin for a beautiful maiden (FGH 76 F5), about a mythical war between Olympias and Eurydice (F52), stories dealing with dress (F14), and about beautiful girls taken as captives to satisfy lust (F18). Phylarchus was often the source for the love stories of Parthenius;[75] one fragment tells of the love of an elephant for a youth (F36), others deal with extravagance in dress and luxury (F44-45), while another tells how springs beneficial to the health of poor people dried up when taxed to obtain money (F66). T. W. Africa has shown the satire behind many of these stories, but there is no doubt that many were also examples of erudite showing off.[76]

Polybius does not use such marvellous stories, and he would seem to lump in with them epiphanic tales. For it is remarkable that, in narrating the repulse of the Gauls from Delphi in 279 B.C.E., he makes no mention at all of the divine help given to the defenders, an epiphany well known in the Greek world.[77] Rather, he lays stress on the moral endurance and the hardihood of the small force of defenders who turn back the invading force (2.35.7). Polybius' focus remains on human political and exemplary history. Herein lies an important distinction from 2 Maccabees. While the author of 2 Maccabees does not use tales of extraordinary animals or narrate entertaining romances and court gossip, he does have at the heart of his message the epiphanic defense of Jerusalem and its territory. His focus is on religious instruction.

The Marvellous Acts of God

Epiphanies play a major role in the structure of the narrative of 2 Maccabees. The programmatic statement in the prologue at 2 Macc 2:21-22 is carried out in the narrative itself, as the first major event is the epiphanic

---

[74] F. W. Walbank, "History and Tragedy," 216.

[75] E.g., the love stories about Daphne (15), Phaullos (25), and Dimoitos (31).

[76] T. W. Africa, *Phylarchus*, 5-8.

[77] See the previous chapter.

repulse of Heliodorus from Jerusalem (3:1-40), the first major victory is won because God fights as the Jews' ally (8:24), and the final battle is won by the epiphany of God (15:27). God is, after all, he who "always aids his own with his epiphanic help" (14:15). As noted in the previous chapter, God is appealed to for help in every conflict. There are, however, four occasons when such help is graphically pictured: 3:24-28; 5:2-4; 10:29-30; 11:8-11. In these scenes, figures appear who help the Jews: they deserve closer attention.

In the Bible, descriptions of divine helpers are found, but not frequently. Before Jericho, Joshua "lifted up his eyes and looked, and behold, a man stood before him with his drawn sword in his hand; and Joshua went up to him and said to him, 'Are you for us, or for our adversaries?' And he said, 'No; but as commander of the army of the Lord I have now come'" (Josh 5:13-14). God's angel is sent against Israel when David takes a census. "And David lifted up his eyes and saw the angel of the Lord standing between heaven and earth, and in his hand a drawn sword stretched out over Jerusalem" (1 Chr 21:16; 2 Sam 24:16-17). More detailed descriptions of heavenly helpers occur in revelatory visions than in battle scenes, e.g., Isaiah 6; Ezekiel 1; Dan 10:4-6; Zech 1:7-11; 6:1-8.

Some Near Eastern accounts where divine help is promised and provided have already been noted.[78] However, it is within Greek literature that descriptions of divine helpers abound, and this forms the immediate backdrop for the descriptions in 2 Maccabees, as the following analysis will show.

1. 3:24-28

This epiphany, with its emphasis on the strength and the beauty of the two young men, on the golden accoutrements of the horse, and the fearful character of the rider, is typical of epiphanies in Greek literature. When the Dioscuri appear to help the Roman army at the see of Regillus, they are described thus:

> It is said that in this battle two men on horseback, far excelling in both beauty and stature those our human stock produces . . . appeared. . . . And after the flight of the Latins and the capture of their camp, the battle having come to an end in the late afternoon, two youths are said to have appeared in the same manner in the Roman Forum attired in their military garb, very tall and beautiful and of the same age, themselves retaining on their countenances the look of combatants, as having come from a battle, and the horses they led being all in a sweat (D. H. 6.13).

[78] See the previous chapter; for a good overview, see E. Pax, art. "Epiphanie," RAC 5.834-835.

Plutarch also reports how tall and comely men brought the news to the Romans (Plu. *Aem. Paul.* 25). Among the gods, one of the epithets was *chrysaoros* = the one with the sword of gold, an epithet of Apollo, but also of Demeter and Zeus.[79]

Throughout this epiphanic description in 2 Macc 3:24-26, then, one can discern the influence of Greek epiphanic descriptions. As noted above, one finds propaganda and a "conversion" motif which have parallels in the Lindos Chronicle.

2. 5:2-4

In this passage, Grimm had already noted the use of technical Greek military terminology, and I noted above the emphasis on golden armor. The whole episode belongs to prodigies which foretell coming events.

> The recording of omens was a traditional feature in the annals of the Romans, and the effect of premonitory signs on the minds and actions of men provided a suitable commentary to great events. Idle fables were to be deprecated, but a serious author had no right to omit a well-authenticated manifestation.[80]

The closest parallels to the passage in 2 Maccabees are those of Josephus as he foretells the coming destruction of Jerusalem: "For before sunset throughout all parts of the country chariots were seen in the air and armed battalions hurtling through the clouds and encompassing the cities" (*J. W.* 6.298); and Pliny:

> We are told that during the wars with the Cimbrians a noise of clanging armor and the sounding of a trumpet were heard from the sky, and that the same thing has happened frequently both before then and after. In the third consulship of Marius, the inhabitants of Ameria and Tuder saw the spectacle of heavenly armies advancing from the East and the West to meet in battle, those from the West being routed (*NH* 2.58).

The passage in 2 Macc 5:2-4 thus belongs to Greco-Roman prodigy literature

---

[79] Homer *Il.* 5.509; 15.256; of Detemer: *h.Cer.* 4;; of Zeus: Strabo 14.2.25. One should note that golden armor was known from the encounter with the Persians: a Persian officer rode a horse with a golden bridle, and wore a golden coreselet under his scarlet tunic (Hdt 9.20 and 22) E. Bickermann ("Héliodore," 25) also suggested that the horse with rearing forefeet is less a attitude of attack than an artist's pose. He quotes Xenophon (*Anab.* 3.2.18) for the statement that no one has ever been killed by a rearing horse in battle, while in *de equit* 11.6 and Xenophon states that gods and heroes are represented on rearing horses.

[80] R. Syme, *Tacitus* (Oxford: Oxford Univ. Press, 1958) 522, paraphrasing Tac *H* 2.50.2; 2.78.2.

3. 10:29-31

In this passage five heavenly figures on horses with golden bridles fight for the Jews and scatter the enemy with their hurled thunderbolts; two protect Judas Maccabeus.[81] In the Iliad, that *locus classicus* of gods fighting with men, the gods often defend their heroes, as, for example, Apollo defends Aineias from Diomedes: "Three times, furious to cut him down, Diomedes drove forward, and three times Apollo battered aside the bright shield" (5.436-437). As to the battle itself in 2 Maccabees, parallels are found in the defense of Delphi against the Persians (Hdt 8.36-39) and the Gauls (Paus 1.4.4; 10.23.1-6). In the account in Herodotus,

> thunderbolts fell on the Persians from the sky, and two pinnacles of rock, torn from Parnassus, came crashing and rumbling down amongst them, killing a large number, while at the same time there was a battle-cry from inside the shrine (Hdt 8.37).

Also, two gigantic soldiers pursued the fleeing barbarians, and they were identified as two local heroes, Phylacus and Autonous (8.38-39). In Pausanius' account, which is influenced by the account of the earlier Persian attack on Delphi, the bolts from heaven "would not only strike a man down, but set fire to other men and their shields all around him" (Paus 10.23.3). Three, or maybe four, divine heroes appeared against the attackers. The next night, panic struck them so that they began to fight one another. This motif of self-slaughter brought on by fear is also present at 2 Macc 12:22.

In the incident at 2 Macc 10:29-31, the use of the word *keraunoi* is noteworthy. It is rare in the LXX, being found only two other times, at Job 38:35 and Wisdom of Solomon 19:13. In Job, the natural phenomenon of lightning is attributed to God; in Wisdom, God sent lightning as a warning sign to the Egyptians to let his people go. However, in the many storm epiphanies of God, *keraunos* is not used. At Sinai, God thunders and peals, but does not throw thunderbolts, although *keraunoi* is found in the account of Josephus *Ant* 3.80. Lightning is described as God's arrows as at Ps 18:14: "And he sent out his arrows, and scattered them; he flashed forth lightnings, and routed them." (Cf. Wis 5:21.) God uses storms to help Israel (Josh 10:10-11; 1 Sam 7:10-11). The term *keraunos*, however, is not used. Rather, it is Zeus who is called *Zeus Keraunos*,[82] who preeminently hurls thunderbolts at his enemies (*Od 23.330*; Hes *Th* 854), as do the gods in defense of Delphi.

---

[81] I retain οἱ δύο with Hanhart and Habicht as the *lectio difficilior*: one can understand why it would have been displaced, but not why it would have been added.

[82] IG 5.288.

The number of divine protectors in 2 Maccabees, five, has so far received no satisfactory explanation.[83] As one can see from the account of Herodotus at Delphi and the tales of the Dioscuri, two was often the number of protectors.

From the appearance of divine helpers who both protect the hero and scatter the enemy in panic with the aid of *keraunoi*, one can see the influence of Greek epiphanic descriptions on the style of the author of 2 Maccabees.

4. 11:8-11

> But there, while they were still near Jerusalem, a rider, clothed in white, appeared at their head, brandishing gold weapons. . . . So they advanced in good order with their heavenly ally, for the Lord had had mercy on them.

As noted above, Joshua meets the commander of the Lord's army before the battle of Jericho (Josh 5:13-15), but the closest parallel is the presence of the Dioscuri at the battle between the Latins and the Romans at Lake Regillus. In the account of Dionysius of Halicarnassus (6.13), they "charged at the head of the Roman horse, striking with their spears all the Latins they encountered and driving them headlong before them." One might suspect that Athena had performed the same service for the citizens of Cyzicus, for she appeared to many in Ilium "with the sweat running down her person, and showed them her robe torn in one place, telling them that she had just arrived from relieving the Cyzicians" (Plu *Lucullus* 10.3). Or Theseus, who, at the battle of Marathon, rushed at the head of the Greeks against the barbarians (Plu *Thes* 35). The role of the divine heroes of the Greeks has in 2 Maccabees been taken over by the angel of the Lord.

From this analysis of the four scenes where divine helpers are described in 2 Maccabees, one can see that the descriptions use the terminology and the same dramatic effects as the Greco-Roman historians. There remains, however, one major difference. Whereas in the Greco-Roman stories it is the god himself or a hero who appears, in the Jewish narrative of 2 Maccabees, it is always the angels of ministers of God who do his work for him.

Such a use of angels is consistent with the growing angelology of the Jews of this period. The Dead Sea Scrolls witness the belief of the presence of angels among men, and the angels of God battle against the angels of

[83] L. Ginzberg, *The Legends of the Jews*, tr. H. Szold (Philadelphia: Jewish Publication Society, 1909-38) 6.251, n.38, suggested Abraham, Issac, Jacob, Moses, and Aaron. Grimm suggested five because of the five sons of Mattathias.

Darkness.[84] What is exciting about 2 Maccabees is that the author has so skillfully taken over the descriptions of interventions of Greek gods and heroes and used them to depict angels. This is another instance of how the author has combined his Jewish faith with his Greek style.

Epiphanic Collections

2 Maccabees, then, is a history of recent events filled with the theme of the epiphanic help of God.

That epiphanies (or aretalogies) of gods were collected is attested by the massive inscription detailing healings wrought by Asclepius,[85] as well as by the epiphanies listed on the Lindos Chronicle. This Chronicle is interesting in that it shows the diversity of aretalogical accounts: the first epiphany deals with the defense of the city and its relief when besieged through an unusual shower of rain—as noted above, it is propaganda for the island; the second epiphany deals with ordinances for the ritual purification of the temple given through a dream appearance of Athena; the third is an appearance of Athena during the siege of the island by Demetrius in 305-304 advising the islanders to send to Ptolemy I for help—clear pro-Egyptian propaganda. What is most interesting is that the author of the Chronicle cites at the end of each epiphany authorities for the narrative. For example, at the end of the first epiphany it is narrated:

> These events are described by Eudemus in his *Lindiaca*, by Ergias in the fourth of his histories, by Polyzelus in the fourth of his histories, by Hieronymus in Book 2 . . . of his *Heliaca*, by Myron in Book 30 of his *Praise of Rhodes*, by Timocritus in Book 1 of his work *On Rhodes*. Xenagoras, in Book 4 of his Chronological Summary, states that the epiphany took place, but he connects it with Mardonius, as the commander sent by Datis. Aristo also mentions the epiphany in Book 30 of his *Chronological Summary*.

At the end of the second epiphany, the authorities of Eudemus, Timocritus, Xenagoras, Onomastus, and Aristonymus are cited. One notices that there are three distinct works specifically on Rhodes which are cited as authorities for the epiphany—the works of Eudemus (FGH 524), Myron

---

[84] 1QM 12.4-7. For the notion of the co-dwelling of the Covenanters with angels, see J. Strugnell, "The Angelic Liturgy at Qumrân: 4Q Serek Šîrôt ʿÔlat Haššabbat," *International Organization for the Study of the Old Testament. 3rd Congress.* (VTSup 7; Leiden: Brill, 1960) 318-345.

[85] For the full text, see V. Longo, *Aretalogie nel Mondo Greco* (Pubblicazioni dell'Istituto di Filologia Classica 29; Genoa: Pagano, 1969) 63-72.

(FGH 106), and Timocritus (FGH 522). Such works must be compared with the activity of another historian, Syriscus of Chersonesus, to whom an inscription was set up honoring him for having written "with much labor, the epiphanies of the Virgin, and given an account of the kings of the Bosporus, and narrated the privileges and immunities which belong to the cities in a way favorable to the city."[86] Such a history probably contained accounts of the epiphanic help given by Athena to Chersonesus during the invasion of the Gauls at the beginning of the 3rd century B.C.E. The repulse of the Gauls from Delphi by Apollo and perhaps other gods, the role of Artemis in repulsing them from Bargylia,[87] the help of Heracles to Cyzicus[88] at this time are all recorded. Syriscus would have incorporated such epiphanies in his history of Chersonesus, as Eudemus, Myron, and Timocritus had done for Rhodes.

2 Maccabees, too, is the history of a city and its territory[89] and its defense by its patron deity. The similarity in situation and detail between it and the excerpts and descriptions of the above works cannot go unnoticed. One cannot speak in terms of a genre, for this self-contained motif cluster of temple-territory threatened/epiphanic deliverance/rejoicing-praising of devotees is *not* a genre. A more accurate term might be topos, since one is dealing with a smaller pattern of elements than would have to be considered in a discussion of genre. But these, roughly contemporaneous works share a rather traditional, expected pattern or theme.[90] This theme is the major contributing thread to the work of 2 Maccabees as a whole. The isolation of such a theme allows one to place the work in proper relation to other works which share such a theme. Such a contextual approach begins with what is actually in 2 Maccabees, rather than with an imprecise lumping of 2 Maccabees with "tragic" historiography, a genre whose very existence is unprovable. In conclusion, 2 Maccabees is a history characteristic of the Hellenistic period which deals with the divine deliverance of Jerusalem and its territory from around 180 to 160 B.C.E. by its patron deity.

---

[86] FGH 807 T 1.

[87] L. Robert, *Études Anatoliennes. Recherches sur les Inscriptions Grecques de l'Asie Mineure* (Études Orientales 5; Paris: E. Boccard, 1937) 459-461.

[88] M. Launey, "Études d'Histoire hellénistique, I," *Revue des études anciennes* 46 (1944) 217-236. For a full catalogue of such epiphanies, see M. Launey, *Recherches sur les Armée hellénistiques* (Bibliothèque des Écoles Françaises d'Athènes et de Rome 169; Paris: E. Boccard, 1949-50)897-901.

[89] B. Renaud, "La Loi et les lois dans les livres des Maccabées," *RB* 68 (1961) 39-52. Cf. D. Arenhoevel, *Theocratie*, 126-129.

[90] As the term is used by A. Lord, *The Singer of Tales* (New York: Atheneum, 1965) 68-98.

The Festal Connection

Once the major theme of 2 Maccabees is seen to be the epiphanic deliverances of Jerusalem and its people, one can place in proper perspective the institution of the two feasts at 10:6 and 15:36. Festivals were often instituted after such deliverances. The repulse of the Gauls from Delphi by Apollo and other gods was celebrated, almost immediately after the victory, with Soteria at Athens, Cos, Chios, Teos, Tenos, and Eritrea.[91] Plutarch recalls how the victory over the Persians at Platea was celebrated with an annual sacrifice to *Zeus Eleutherios*.[92] Castor and Pollux were honored annually by the Romans for their help in defeating the Latins at the Lake Regillus battle.[93] The annual feasts set up to celebrate the purification of the altar and the victory over Nicanor are to be expected after such epiphanic deliverances. The straightforward proclamation of the feasts by the author, with no elaboration of the ceremonies entailed, supports this.

One should not, therefore, approach the narrative of 2 Maccabees as a "festal legend." J. G. Bunge and A. Momigliano have recently attempted to do so.[94] From Greco-Roman literature, Momigliano brings forward the *Atthides* and Ovid's *Fasti* as examples of such a genre of "Festlegende." These comparisons are not valid, however. From what is known of the *Atthides*, they attempt to provide a chronological treatment of a city from its founding in mythological times to the present. They deal not only with religious institutions, but also with the political constitution of the city. Finally, their discussion of religious institutions is dominated by etiological explanations of why a feast is celebrated and performed in a certain way. A good example is provided by Phanodemus in his discussion of the institution of the Dionysic Feast of Pitchers:

> As for the Feast of Pitchers celebrated at Athens, Phanodemus says that King Demophon instituted it when he desired to entertain Orestes on his arrival at Athens. Since Demophon did not wish Orestes to be admitted at the holy rites, or share in the libations when he had not as yet been tried, Demophon ordered the sacred utensils to be locked up, and a pitcher of wine to be set before each participant, saying that a flat-cake would be given to the one who drank out his pitcher first. He

---

[91] For a full discussion both of the literary and epigraphical accounts, see G. Nachtergael, *Les Galates en Grèce*.

[92] Plu *Aristides* 20.4; for the sacrifices offered, see 21.1-3.

[93] D.H. 6.13.

[94] J. G. Bunge, *Untersuchungen*, 184-190; A. Momigliano, "The Second Book of Maccabees," *Classical Philology* 70 (1975) 81-88. Before Momigliano, M. Hadas had compared these various works to one another in his commentary on 3 and 4 Maccabees (*The Third and Fourth Books of Maccabees* [New York: Harper, 1953] 6-16).

also ordered that after they had finished the drinking they should not place the wreaths they had been wearing near the sacred images, since they had been under the same roof as Orestes, but that everyone should twine his wreath round his own pitcher and the priestess should carry away the wreaths to the sacred precinct in the Marshes, and then complete the sacrifices in the temple. Since that time the festival has been called the "Pitchers."[95]

Philochorus in his work discussed how Amphictyon instituted the worship of the nymphs as daughters of Dionysus, and how Erichtonius was the one who introduced the custom that maidens should carry baskets and old men olive branches in the Panathenic procession. These are etiological explanations of the ritual of the feasts.[96] Besides the fact that the *Atthides* and 2 Maccabees involve feasts in some way, there is no connection between the works.[97] As for Ovid's *Fasti*, this is a poem that works through the Roman calendar of feasts, also seeking etiologies for the ways in which different festivals are celebrated and for their divergent customs. To crown all, the *Fasti* are in some sense set in the form of a revelatory vision: Ovid, struggling to understand the Roman calendar, is rewarded first by a vision of Janus who explains the origins and customs of the feasts of his month. How can one speak of a similarity of genre between this work and 2 Maccabees?

Both Bunge and Momigliano point to the Book of Esther as another example of a "Festlegende," a comparison which M. Hadas had also produced. Since both Bunge and Momigliano include the introductory letters as written by the author of the narrative as a kind of introduction, 2 Maccabees would also have in common with Esther letters instituting the feast. First, however, the description of Esther as a festal legend relies on an assumption about the unity of Esther, an assumption which has been seriously questioned by a number of scholars. Barucq and Würthwein suggest that Esther originally ended at 9:19; Esther 9:20-10 and the etymology of Purim in 3:7 would have been added later to the narrative.[98] The strongly festal character of Esther, therefore, may well be secondary. Secondly, elements of the narrative in Esther differ markedly from elements in the epitome. Esther and Mordecai trumph over Haman by their wisdom in court confrontations

---

[95] Athenaeus, *Deipnosophistae*, 10.437 cd.

[96] See L. Pearson, *The Local Historians of Attica* (Philological Monographs published by the American Philological Association 11; Philadelphia: Lancaster, 1942) 112-113.

[97] For a discussion of the *Atthides*, and particularly their relation to political matters see, besides the work of Pearson just cited, F. Jacoby, *Attis; the local chronicles of ancient Athens* (Oxford: Clarendon, 1949).

[98] A. Barucq, *Judith. Esther* (La Sainte Bible; Paris: Cerf, 1959) 89; E. Würthwein, *Die fünf Megilloth. Ruth, das Hohelied, Esther* (HAT 18/1; Tübingen: Mohr, 1969) 171-172.

rather than by divine intervention in pitched battles. There are no martyrdoms in Esther, but rather the clever heroes win the court contest, as Talmon
has shown,[99] through the application of proverbial wisdom. There are no
didactic reflections or excursuses in Esther. Except for the Greek Additions,
there are no hints in Esther of Greek rhetorical style. Given these contrasts in
style and content and given the redactional difficulties in asserting that
Esther is a festal legend at all, the consideration of 2 Maccabees and Esther
as examples of the same literary genre fails.[100] The presence of a feast is
not enough to constitute a genre, or one would have to see Exodus as a
"festal legend."

There are, however, similarities between Esther and 2 Maccabees, as
noted above. There is a surprising congruence of language between the
accusations made by Haman and the king in his decree against the Jews as
an unsociable people and the accusations against the Jews in 2 Maccabees.
One also has to note that in both books only defensive measures are taken
against the heathens. The Jews defend their right to exist as a people, but
they do not go beyond these measures. This is true of Esth 8:11, which has
often been misinterpreted. As R. Gordis has shown, the verse should be
rendered: "By these letters the king permitted the Jews in every city to gather
and defend themselves, to destroy, kill and wipe out every armed force of a
people or province attacking 'them, their children and their wives, with their
goods as booty.'"[101] The last five words in the Hebrew text are a citation of
Haman's original edict. The Jews are not given permission to take revenge,
but to defend themselves, their wives and children. The Jews are good citizens, and both Esther and Mordecai have shown great service to the king.

A similar emphasis is found in 3 Maccabees. In this work, the Jews'
loyalty is stressed, and it is stated that some Greeks were sympathetic to the
plight of the Jews and tried to protect them (3 Macc 3:8-10). Similarities in
language between 2 and 3 Maccabees on this theme of the sociability of the
Jews have been noted above. In contrast to Esther and the other parallels
adduced, 3 Maccabees has epiphanic deliverances and feasts are introduced
to celebrate some of them (3 Macc 6:36). There is thus a close link between 2
and 3 Maccabees in theme as well as language and style. This is particularly
true of the repulse of Ptolemy from the temple of Jerusalem and the repulse
of Heliodorus. However, there are significant differences. The central problem of 3 Maccabees is the question of the good citizenship of the Jews. This

---

[99] S. Talmon, "Wisdom in the Book of Esther," *VT* 13 (1963) 419-455.

[100] One should note, in fact, that some scholars maintain that an older version of Esther
as revised in the Maccabean period from the Maccabean point of view. See J. C. H. Lebram,
"Purimfest und Estherbuch," *VT* 22 (1972) 208-222.

[101] R. Gordis, "Studies in the Esther Narrative," *JBL* 95 (1976) 51-52.

can be seen from the first comments of the king after the Jews have been miraculously delivered:

> For when he heard the outcry and saw them all prostrate to meet their death, he wept and angrily threatened his friends, saying "You usurp the kingly power, and you surpass the tyrants in cruelty; you are even endeavoring to deprive me, your benefactor, of my rule and even of my life, secretly contriving, as you do, measures disadvantageous to my kingship. Who has driven from their homes those who faithfully kept our country's strongholds, and gathered them, every one, here? Who has so unlawfully overwhelmed with indignities those who from the beginning have been more conspicuous than all peoples in their good will toward us, and who have frequently encountered mankind's worst dangers on our behalf? Loose their unjust bonds, loose them utterly. . . . Set free the children of the Almighty and heavenly living God, who from the days of our ancestors until now has conferred upon our estate unimpaired stability and glory (3 Macc 6:22-28).

The epiphany of 3 Macc 6:18-21 is, in fact, out of place as 6:22 shows. God is called upon to make his epiphanic presence known, but he does this through sleep (5:11-12), forgetfulness (5:27-28), and repentance (6:22), as well as the epiphanies of 2:21-24 and 6:18-20. Like Esther, 3 Maccabees is the story of the unjustified hatred of one man towards the Jews, who are loyal citizens; unlike Esther, but like 2 Maccabees, the problem is resolved through divine intervention. 2 Maccabees, therefore, has as its major theme the epiphanic deliverance of the Jews, with a minor theme being the fact that the Jews are good social citizens. 3 Maccabees has as its major theme the fact that the Jews are good citizens, with a minor theme being the epiphanic help of God. Finally, one must note that the main action of 3 Maccabees takes place in Alexandria and in Egypt. While the temple at Jerusalem is the scene for the first arrogant behavior of Ptolemy and Ptolemy does threaten to burn it with fire and make it desolate (5:43), the temple does not occupy the central position in 3 Maccabees that it does in 2 Maccabees. 3 Maccabees is a story for the diaspora, those in sojourn (6:36; 7:19). In 2 Maccabees, Judea is the temple territory of Jerusalem and it is that that God defends as its patron deity.

Conclusion

The analysis so far has enabled one to place the work of 2 Maccabees in proper relation to the remains of the literature of its time. Such a perspective highlights the astonishing feat that the author has achieved. He has maintained intact the themes of his Jewish religion while assimilating holus-bolus the literary forms of his gentile neighbors. This is a remarkable achievement. It is much more successful than the clumsy attempt of Artapanus to retell the patriarchal narratives. The author deserves proper recognition for his work.

CONCLUSION

What emerges from the literary analysis of 2 Maccabees? First and foremost is the Deuteronomic theme that the invincible God of the Jews protects his temple and his people only when they are loyal to him and good. Next, the author does not share the apocalyptic vision of the establishment of a new order of reality—he ends his narrative with the Hebrews in control of Jerusalem, but the threat remains, and it is explicitly stated in the excursuses 5:17-20; 6:12-17 that this situation could change if the Jews fall away from their God. The author does not expect God to alter radically the mode of earthly existence now, but after death a radical change occurs with the individual resurrection of the righteous.[1] The readiness for martyrdom and the belief in individual resurrection are not opposed to the theme of God as Divine Warrior, as Momigliano would seem to say,[2] but they complement it.

The decisive threat to Jewish sovereignty thus comes from inside the Jewish nation: the wicked Simon, the dastardly Jason, Menelaus, and Lysimachus, the traitor Rhodocus, the unscrupulous Alcimus as well as the venal followers of Simon Maccabeus and the image-wearers who fall against Gorgias—these raise the threat to the Jews, for they show disobedience to God. Without this inner falling-away, the Jews would be invincible. The aping of foreign ways, the running to the gymnasium, the overthrow of the ancestral laws can only lead to destruction. By way of digression, it is interesting to see this author, obviously well-educated in Greek style, railing against Greek ways, much as Jerome would rail against classical literature and yet use it to the hilt for his own polemic. The author of the epitome insists on keeping Jewish ways intact, and stresses that his heroes speak Hebrew. His whole work is Temple-oriented. The epitome, in this sense, calls for a re-dedication to the cultural values of Judaism.

Such nationalism, however, is not hostile to non-Jews. The author distinguishes between good and bad Greeks (4:35-36.49; Ptolemy Macron

---

[1] On the notion of resurrection in 2 Maccabees, see U. Kellermann, *Auferstanden in den Himmel. 2 Makkabäer 7 und die Auferstehung der Märtyrer* (SBS 95; Stuttgart: Katholisches Bibelwerk, 1979). H. C. C. Cavallin (*Life After Death* [Lund: CWK Gleerup, 1974] 111-116) notes that nothing is said about the date of the expected resurrection in 2 Maccabees; however, the insistence on the receiving back of one's own limbs (7:11; 14:46) suggests individual resurrection, and the speech of the mother suggests immediate comfort (7:29).

[2] A. Momigliano, "The Second Book," 86-87.

10:12-13; the citizens of Scythopolis 12:30). The author shows no embar-
rassment that the high-priest Onias sought asylum at the temple area of
Daphne (4:33), nor does he blush at connections with the Macedonians (5:9)
or rule out that Jews be equated with Athenians (9:15); he emphasizes connections with the Romans (4:11; 11:34-38). The theme that the Jews are good
citizens, not barbarians like those who attack them (2:21), is also part-and-
parcel of this openness to non-Jews.

The portrait thus emerges of a man who wishes to maintain solid
diplomatic ties with other nations and cities, and who insists that Jews
follow their own ancestral laws and be proud of them, a conservative who is
not blind to world political realities, nor a fanatic. I suggest that he belongs
to that educated group, influenced by Hellenism but loyal to Judaism, in
which Ben Sira and Eupolemus would have felt at home.[3]

Date:

When did such a man write his work, the epitome? Dates suggested
range from the 2nd cent. B.C.E. to the 1st cent. C.E.[4] Habicht renounces the
attempt.[5] Momigliano has recently connected the epitome with the date of
the first letter: he suggests that an official of the Jerusalem council, when
asked to invite the Egyptian Jews to celebrate the 25th Kislev, transcribed a
letter attributed to Judas and also asked a writer to make a summary of
Jason's work.[6] The epitome would therefore be dated to 124 B.C.E. Momigliano notes the major objection against the theory: there is no mention of such
a purpose in the preface of the epitome where one would expect it.[7] Rather, I
suggested above that the first letter shows signs of editing to align it with the
epitome. I also noted the thematic and linguistic relationships between
2 Maccabees and 3 Maccabees and the Additions B and E of Esther. Since
these themes are woven in the very fabric of 2 Maccabees, and are not

---

[3] I am not suggesting the existence of another formalized political party, but rather
an attitude.

For Ben Sira, see Th. Middendorp, *Die Stellung Jesu Ben Siras zwischen Judentum und
Hellenismus* (Leiden: Brill, 1973); J. Marbock, *Weisheit im Wandel: Untersuchungen zur Weis-
heitstheologie bei Ben Sira* (BBB 37; Bonn: Hanstein, 1971).

For Eupolemus, see N. Walter, *Fragmente jüdisch-hellenistischer Historiker* (JRSHRZ
1.2; Gütersloh: G. Mohn, 1976); B.Z. Wacholder, *Eupolemus: A Study of Judaeo-Greek Literature* (Cincinnati: Hebrew Union College, 1974).

[4] As throughout this study, I have renounced efforts to find what were the emphases of
Jason of Cyrene—one simply cannot isolate and recover the complete outline of Jason's work
from the epitome; so here I will not try to date Jason's work.

[5] C. Habicht, *2 Makkabäerbuch*, 169-170.

[6] A. Momigliano, "The Second Book," 83.

[7] A. Momigliano, "The Second Book," 83-84.

additions to the text, I hold that 3 Maccabees and Additions B and E of Esther show the influence of 2 Maccabees. However, since there is no scholarly consensus as to the date of these last works, this does not provide secure footing either.[8] A strong argument is that the author of the epitome could not have written 2 Macc 15:37 nor maintained a friendly attitude to the Romans after Pompey's entry into Jerusalem in 63 B.C.E.; but he could have been a priestly follower of Hyrcanus II and Antipater, so this dating is not secure either.

Can one be more precise? The epitome, as just noted, contains a threat against adopting foreign ways and a desire to show the Jews as respecters of the rights of Gentile sovereigns and cities. These two policies were threatened during the reign of John Hyrcanus. In 129 B.C.E. after the death of Antiochus VII, Hyrcanus I began a vigorous territorial expansion which included the forcible circumcision of the Idumeans (Jos *Ant* 13.257). The attitude of the Jews under Judas, as portrayed in 2 Maccabees, is in direct contrast to Hyrcanus' policy: Judas and his men only fight when attacked. The decision of Hyrcanus I to maintain mercenaries would be counter to the opinion of the author of 2 Maccabees to rely on God;[9] his plundering of the tomb of David (Jos *J. W.* 1.61; *Ant* 13.249) might recall Menelaus' plundering of the temple plate to pay for his position (2 Macc 4:32.39). The positions advocated by the author of 2 Maccabees go against those adopted by Hyrcanus, son of Simon—and it is noteworthy that Simon is peculiarly blundering and incompetent in 2 Maccabees (10:20-22; 14:17). I would suggest, then that 2 Maccabees may point to the existence of a policy debate during the early years of Hyrcanus I. Such a debate, I believe, would be more plausible grounds for Hyrcanus' rift with the Pharisaic "party" than that assigned by Josephus (*Ant* 13.288-297).[10]

The epitome, following this reasoning, would have been written during the early years of John Hyrcanus I.[11] I see no reason to suppose the epitome

---

[8]   On Additions B and E of Esther, see Carey A. Moore, *Daniel, Esther and Jeremiah: The Additions* (AB 44; Garden City, NY: Doubleday, 1977) 161.165-166.

[9]   Does the event in 2 Macc 12:32-45 where some Jews fall in battle because of wearing idol amulets around their necks evidence a general reaction against any foreign, i.e., impure, element in God's army?

[10]   It is interesting that in Josephus (*Ant* 13.291) the leader against Hyrcanus is called Eleazar, although in the doublet of the story in *b. Qidd.* 66a Eleazar is the supporter of the king, called there Alexander Jannaeus.

[11]   J. A. Goldstein (*I Maccabees*, 64-89) also presents 2 Maccabees (actually, Jason of Cyrene's work) as polemic against the Hasmoneans, and more precisely a polemic against 1 Maccabees. This theory, particularly as regards chronology, is too complex to refute here at length; suffice it to say that it depends more on what Jason (sic!) and 1 Maccabees do *not* say, than on what they do say. My methodological approach is quite different.

to have been written outside Jerusalem: its Greek style is no argument against composition in Jerusalem, and the fervor for the Jerusalem temple is a strong argument for it.[12]

The Addition to the Letters:

I have already noted the connections that can be made between the prefixed letters and the epitome—both the letters and the epitome emphasize the feast of purification and the divine protection afforded the Jews. The festal notice provides the ground for connecting the letters to the epitome. When this was done is difficult to assess—I propose that it was after 124 B.C.E. because of the cryptic nature of the first letter. I would agree with Goldstein that the linking of festal letters with a narrative is common to both Esther and 2 Maccabees,[13] but I would not be quite so sanguine that this means that the letters were prefixed to the epitome after the Greek translation of Esther appeared and in imitation of it. Why could the situation in 2 Maccabees not be due to the storing practices at Jewish archives?

One element which has been overlooked in the discussion is the way in which the addition of the letters changes the message of the epitome. The first letter does not effect such a change, but what of the second letter? One of the themes noticed in the second letter which is not found in the epitome is that of the hope for an ingathering of the people to take place soon (2 Macc 2:18). Such an eschatological hope, found repeatedly in the letter, nuances the stark historical, this-worldly account of the epitome. As the work now stands, the motif of the ingathering of God's people fills out the motif-cluster associated with the victory of the Divine Warrior found in the epitome.

---

[12] As against S. Zeitlin ("The names Hebrew, Jew, and Israel. A Historical Study," *JQR* 43 [1953] 365-379), I do not hold that the use of the term "Hebrew" at 2 Macc 7:31; 11:13; 15:37 means the epitome was written at Antioch. The main proof for Zeitlin lies in the use of the term throughout 4 Macabees. However, 4 Maccabees is an encomium praising and lauding the efforts of the Maccabean martyrs as true descendants of Abraham (6:17.22; 9:21; 15:20.28; 17:6; 18.1.20.23); the author therefore uses the laudatory and archaising title "Hebrew" as part of his elevated style (4:11; 5:2; 8:2; 9:6.18; 17:9) and not the more common term "Jew," which Antiochus IV uses in a derogatory fashion (5:7). Note the use in Artapanus (FGH 726 F1; Eusebius *Praep. Ev.* 9.18.1) where "Hebrew" means "descendant of Abraham." So too in 2 Maccabees, the term is laudatory one: at 7:31, the youngest child extols his nation over against Antiochus IV; at 11:13, the author uses a laudatory term when Lysias recognizes the invicibility of the Hebrews' God; at 15:37, the author ends in praising the achievement with God's help in restoring the temple. The term "Hebrew" is therefore not significant as an indicator of Syrian diaspora vs. Palestinian Jew.

[13] J. A. Goldstein, *I Maccabees*, 551-557.

Conclusion:

With this literary completion, one comes back to the central theme of 2 Maccabees. It is primarily temple propaganda—the defense of the temple and its surroundings by the patron deity. But religion reflects and influences the political and the social. By downplaying the heroism of the Maccabean family, by upgrading the role of pious observers of the Law, and by placing God as the truly decisive actor in the divine drama, the author provides his readers with the proper religious perspective from which they can assess their present leaders.

BIBLIOGRAPHY

Commentaries and Major Reference Works

Abel, F. M. *Les Livres des Maccabées*. EBib. Paris: Gabalda, 1949.

————. and Starcky, J. *Les Livres des Maccabées*. 3rd ed. Paris: Cerf, 1961.

Blass, F., Debrunner, A., and Funk, R.W. *A Greek Grammar of the New Testament and other Early Christian Literature*. Chicago: University of Chicago Press, 1961.

Grimm, C. L. W. *Zweites Buch der Maccabäer*. Kurzgefasstes exegetisches Handbuch zu den Apokryphen des Alten Testamentes. Leipzig: S. Hirzel, 1857.

Goldstein, J. A. *I Maccabees*. AB 41. Garden City, NY: Doubleday, 1976.

Habicht, C. *2 Makkabäerbuch*. Jüdische Schriften aus hellenistisch-römischer Zeit, Band 1, Lfg. 3. Gütersloh: G. Mohn, 1976.

Hanhart, R. (ed.) *Maccabaeorum Liber II*. Vetus Testamentum Graecum IX/2. Göttingen: Vandenhoeck & Ruprecht, 1959.

Kühner, R., and Blass, F. *Ausführliche Grammatik der griechischen Sprache*. 3rd ed. Hanover: Hahn, 1890-1892.

Kühner, R. and Gerth, B. *Ausführliche Grammatik der griechischen Sprache*. Hanover/Leipzig: Hahn, 1898-1904.

de Lagarde, P. A. *Libri Veteris Testamenti Apocryphi Syriace*. Leipzig: Brockhaus, 1861.

Mayser, E. *Grammatik der griechischen Papyri aus der Ptolemäerzeit*. 2nd ed. Berlin: de Gruyter, 1923-1934.

Moulton, J. H. *A Grammar of New Testament Greek*. Vol. I. Edinburgh: T. & T. Clark, 1976.

————. and Howard, W. F. *A Grammar of New Testament Greek*. Vol. II. Edinburgh: T. & T. Clark, 1976.

————. and Turner, N. *A Grammar of New Testament Greek*. Vol. III. Edinburgh: T. & T. Clark, 1976.

————. and Turner, N. *A Grammar of New Testament Greek*. Vol. IV. Edinburgh: T. & T. Clark, 1976.

Preisigke, F., and Kiessling, E. *Wörterbuch der griechischen Papyrusurkunden*. Berlin: Selbtsverlag der Erben, 1925-1931.

Thackeray, H. St. John. *A Grammar of the Old Testament in Greek according to the Septuagint*. Vol. I. Cambridge: Cambridge Univ. Press, 1909.

For the classical authors, I have used the Teubner edition of the Greek text and LCL translation, unless otherwise stated.

Other Works

Abel, F. M. "Topographie des Campagnes Maccabéennes," *RB* 32 (1923) 495-521; 33 (1924) 201-217; 371-387; 34 (1925) 194-210; 35 (1926) 206-222; 510-533.

―――. "Les lettres preliminaires du second livre des Maccabées," *RB* 53 (1946) 513-533.

Adinolfi, M. *Questioni Bibliche di Storia e Storiografia*. Brescia: Paideia, 1969.

Africa, T. W. *Phylarchus and the Spartan Revolution*. University of California Publications in History 68. Berkeley/Los Angeles: Univ. of California Press, 1961.

Arenhoevel, D. *Die Theokratie nach dem 1. und 2. Makkabäerbuch*. Mainz: Matthias-Gruenwald-Verlag, 1967.

Avenarius, G. *Lukians Schrift zur Geschichtsschreibung:* Meisenheim/Glan: Hain, 1956.

Avi-Yonah, M. "'War of the Sons of Light and the Sons of Darkness' and the Maccabean Warfare," *IEJ* 2 (1952) 1-5.

Bardtke, H. *Das Buch Esther*. KAT XVII/4-5. Göttersloh: G. Mohn, 1963.

Barucq, A. *Judith. Esther*. La Sainte Bible; Paris: Cerf, 1959.

Beek, M. A. "Relations entre Jérusalem et la Diaspora égyptienne au 2ᵉ siècle avant J.-C," *OTS* 2 (1943) 119-143.

Benseler, G. E. *De Hiatu in Oratoribus Atticis et Historicis Graecis*. Freiburg: J.G. Engelhardt, 1841.

Bertram, G. "παιδεύω," in *TDNT* 5.596-625.

Bickermann, E. "The Colophon of the Greek Book of Esther," *JBL* 63 (1944) 339-362.

―――. *Studies in Jewish and Christian History. Part 1*. AGJU 9; Leiden: Brill, 1976.

―――. "Héliodore au Temple de Jérusalem," *Annuaire de l'Institut de Philologie et d'Histoire Orientales et Slaves* 7 (1939-1944) 5-40.

―――. "Ein jüdischer Festbrief vom Jahre 124 v. Chr. (2 Makk 1, 1-9)," *ZNW* 32 (1933) 233-253.

―――. *Institutions des Seleucides*. Paris: P. Geuthner, 1938.

Birke, O. *De particularum μή et οὐ usu Polybiano Dionysiaco Diodoreo Straboniano*. Leipzig: O. Schmidt, 1897.

Blinkenberg, C. "Die Lindische Tempelchronik," *Kleine Texte für Vorlesungen und Übungen* 31. Bonn: A. Marcus & E. Weber, 1915.

Bott, H. *De Epitomis Antiquis*. Marpurgi Chattorum: J. Hamel, 1920.

Breasted, J. H. *Ancient Records of Egypt*. Chicago: Univ. of Chicago Press, 1906.

Brief, S. *Die Conjunctionen bei Polybius*. Vienna: Verlag des k. k. Staatsgymnasiums im XVII Bezirke von Wien (Hernals), 1891-94.

―――. "Wie beeinflusst die Vermeidung des Hiatus den Stil des Polybius?" in *Dreiundfünfzigster Jahresbericht des k. k. deutschen Staats-Obergymnasium in Un.-Hradisch für das Schuljahr 1906-1907*. (Ungarisch-Hradisch: Verlag des k. k. deutschen Staats-Obergymnasiums, 1907) 3-20.

Brownlee, W. H. "Maccabees, Books of," in *IDB*. Vol. 3. ed. G. A. Buttrick; New York: Abingdon, 1962.

Bruston, C. "Trois lettres des Juifs de Palestine," *ZAW* 10 (1890) 110-117.

De Bruyne, D. "Le text grec du deuxième des Maccabées," *RB* 39 (1930) 503-519.

Büchler, A. *Die Tobiaden und die Oniaden im II. Makkabäerbuch und in der verwandten jüdisch-hellenistischen Literatur*. Vienna: Verlag der Israel.-theol. Lehranstalt, 1899.

Bunge, J. G. *Untersuchungen zum 2. Makkabäerbuch. Quellenkritische, literarische, chronologische, und historische Untersuchungen zum 2 Makkabäerbuch als Quelle syrisch-palästinensischer Geschichte im 2. Jh. v. Chr*. Bonn: Rheinische Friedrich-Wilhelms-Universität, 1971.

_____. "Zu Geschichte und Chronologie des Untergangs der Oniaden und des Aufstiegs der Hasmonäer," *JSJ* (1975) 1-46.

Chantraine, P. *Histoire du Parfait Grec*. Collection Linguistique publiée par la Société de Linguistique de Paris 21. Paris: H. Champion, 1927.

Collins, J. J. *The Sibylline Oracles of Egyptian Judaism*. SBLDS 13. Missoula: Scholars Press, 1974.

Connor, W. R. *Theopompus and fifth-century Athens*. Washington, DC: Centre for Hellenistic Studies, 1968.

Coote, R. B. "Hosea XII," *VT* 21 (1971) 389-402.

Cross, F. M. "The Divine Warrior in Israel's Early Cult," in *Biblical Motifs. Origins and Transformations* (ed. A. Altman; Cambridge: Harvard University Press, 1966) 11-30.

Davies, P. "*Hasidim* in the Maccabean Period," *JJS* 28 (1977) 127-140.

Delcor, M. "Le Temple d'Onias en Egypte," *RB* 75 (1968) 188-205.

Dörrie, H. *Der Königskult des Antiochos von Commagene im Lichte neuer Inschriften-Funde*. Göttingen: Vandenhoeck & Ruprecht, 1964.

Doran, R. "2 Maccabees and 'Tragic History,'" *HUCA* 50 (1979) 107-114.

_____. "The Martyr: A Synoptic View of the Mother and Her Seven Sons," *Ideal Figures in Ancient Judaism: Profiles and Paradigms* (eds. John Collins & George Nickelsburg; Chico: Scholars Press, 1980) 189-221.

Downing, J. "Jesus and Martyrdom," *JTS* 14 (1963) 279-293.

Eddy, S. K. *The King is Dead, studies in the near Eastern resistance to Hellenism, 334-31 B.C*. Lincoln: Univ. of Nebraska Press, 1961.

Exler, F. X. J. *The Form of the Ancient Greek Letter: A Study in Greek Epistolography*. Washington: Catholic University Press, 1923.

Faure, P. "La conduite des armées perses à Rhodes pendant la première guerre médique," *Revue historique* 192 (1941) 236-241.

Fitzmyer, J. A. "Some Notes on Aramaic Epistolography," *JBL* 93 (1974) 201-225.

de Foucault, J. A. *Recherches sur la Langue et le Style de Polybe*. Paris: Société d'Édition "Les Belles Lettres," 1972.

von Fritz, K. "Die Bedeutung des Aristoteles für die Geschichtsschreibung," *Histoire et Historiens dans l'Antiquité* (Fondation Hardt, Entretiens IV; Vandoeuvres-Genève, 1956) 85-128.

————. *Aristotle's Contribution to the practice and theory of historiography*. Berkeley: Univ. of California Press, 1958.

Gabba, E. "Studi su Filarco. Le Biografie plutarchee di Agide e di Cleomene (Capp. I-IV)," *Athenaeum* 35 (1957) 3-55; 193-239.

Galdi, M. *L'epitome nella letteratura latina*. Naples: P. Frederico & G. Ardia, 1922.

Gil, L. "Sobre el estilo de libro 2 de los Macabeos," *Emérita* 26 (1958) 11-32.

Ginzberg, L. *The Legends of the Jews*, trans. H. Szold. Philadelphia: Jewish Publication Society of America, 1909-1938.

Giovannini, G. "The Connection between Tragedy and History in Ancient Criticism," *Philological Quarterly* 22 (1943) 308-314.

Goldstein, J. A. *I Maccabees*. AB 41. Garden City, NY: Doubleday, 1976.

————. "The Tales of the Tobiads," in *Christianity, Judaism, and other Greco-Roman Cults*. Vol. 3 Festschrift for M. Smith, ed. J. Neusner (Leiden: Brill, 1975) 85-123.

Gordis, R. "Studies in the Esther Narrative," *JBL* 95 (1976) 43-58.

de Groot, A. W. *A Handbook of Antique Prose-Rhythm*. Leipzig: Harrassowitz, 1926.

Habicht, C. *Gottmenschentum und griechische Städte*. 3rd ed. Zetemata: Monographien zur klassischen Altertumswissenschaft 14. Munich: Beck, 1970.

————. *2 Makkabäerbuch*. Jüdische Schriften aus hellenistisch-römisch Zeit. Band I, Lfg. 3. Gütersloh: G. Mohn, 1976.

————. "Royal Documents in Maccabees II," *Harvard Studies in Classical Philology* 80 (1976) 1-18.

Hanhart, R. *Zum text des 2. und 3. Makkabäerbuches. Probleme der Überlieferung, der Auslegung und der Ausgabe*. Nachrichten der Akademie der Wissenschaften in Göttingen I. Philologisch-historische Klasse, 1961, no. 13. Göttingen: Vandenhoeck & Ruprecht, 1961.

————. *Zur Zeitrechnung des I und II Makkabäerbuches*. BZAW 88/2. Berlin: Töpelman, 1964.

Heinemann, I. "Synkrisis oder äussere Analogie in der 'Weisheit Salomonos'," *ThZ* 4 (1948) 241-251.

Helbing, R. *Die Kasussyntax der Verba bei den Septuaginta*. Göttingen: Vandenhoeck & Ruprecht, 1928.

Hengel, M. *Judaism and Hellenism: Studies in their encounter in Palestine during the Early Hellenistic Period*, trans. by J. Bowden. Philadelphia: Fortress, 1974.

————. *Juden, Griechen und Barbaren. Aspekte der Hellenisierung des Judentums in vorchristlicher Zeit*. SBS 76. Stuttgart: Katholisches Bibelwerk, 1976.

Jacoby, F. *Atthis; the local chronicles of ancient Athens*. Oxford: Clarendon, 1949.

Kälker, F. "Quaestiones de elocutione Polybiana et de hiatu in libris Diodori Siculi," *Leipziger Studien zur classischen Philologie 3* (Leipzig: S. Hirzel, 1880) 217-320.

Katz, P. "The text of 2 Maccabees Reconsidered," *ZNW* 51 (1960) 10-30.

_____. "Eleazar's Martyrdom in 2 Maccabees: The Latin Evidence for a Point of the Story," *Studia Patristica IV*=Texte und Untersuchungen zur Geschichte der altchristlichen Literatur 79. (Berlin: Akademie-Verlag, 1961) 118-124.

Kebric, R. B. *In the Shadow of Macedon: Duris of Macedon.* Historia Einzelschriften 29. Wiesbaden: F. Steiner, 1977.

Keil, B. "Zur Tempelchronik von Lindos," *Hermes* 51 (1916) 491-498.

Kern, O. *Die Inschriften von Magnesia am Maeander.* Berlin: W. Spemann, 1900.

Knox, B. M. W. "Silent Reading in Antiquity," *Greek, Roman, and Byzantine Studies* 9 (1968) 421-435.

Krebs, F. "Die Präpositionen bei Polybius," *Beiträge zur historischen Syntax der griechischen Sprache*, ed. M. Schanz. (Würzburg: A. Stüber, 1882) 1. 1-147.

Kutscher, E. Y. "The Languages of the Hebrew and Aramaic Letters of Bar Cocheba and his Contemporaries," *Lĕš* 25 (1961) 117-133; 26 (1962) 7-23 (in Hebrew).

Laistner, M. G. *The Greater Roman Historians.* Sather Classical Lectures 21. Berkeley. Univ. of California Press, 1947.

Laqueur, R. *Kritische Untersuchungen zum zweiten Makkabäerbuch.* Strassburg: K. J. Trübner, 1904.

Launey, M. "Études d'Histoire hellénistique, I," *Revue des Études Anciennes* 46 (1944) 217-236.

_____. *Recherches sur les Armées hellénistiques.* Bibliothèque des Écoles Françaises d'Athènes et de Rome 169. Paris: E Boccard, 1949-1950.

Lebram, J. C. H. "Purimfest und Estherbuch," *VT* 22 (1972) 208-222.

Levy, I. "Notes d'Histoire hellénistique sur le second Livre des Maccabées," *Annuaire de l'Institut de Philologie et d'Histoire Orientales et Slaves* 10 (1950) 681-699.

Liebermann, S. *Greek in Jewish Palestine.* New York: Jewish Theological Seminary of America, 1950.

_____. *Hellenism in Jewish Palestine.* New York: Jewish Theological Seminary of America, 1950.

Loftus, F. "The Martyrdom of the Galilean Troglodytes: A Suggested Traditionsgeschichte," *JQR* 66 (1976) 212-223.

Longo, V. *Aretalogie nel Mondo Greco. I. Epigrafi e Papiro.* Genoa: Isituto di Filologia Classica e Medioevale, 1969.

Magnien, V. *Le Futur Grec.* Paris: H. Champion, 1912.

Mandilaras, B. G. *Studies in the Greek Language.* Athens: N. Xenopoulos, 1972.

Mayer-G'Schrey, R. *Parthenius Nicaeensis quale in Fabularum Amatoriarum Breviario dicendi genus secutus sit.* Heidelberg: C. Winter, 1898.

Meecham, H. G. *The Letter of Aristeas. A Linguistic Study with special reference to the Greek Bible.* Manchester: Manchester Univ. Press, 1935.

Meister, K. *Historische Kritik bei Polybios.* Palingenesia 9. Wiesbaden: F. Steiner, 1975.

Miller, P. D. *The Divine Warrior in Early Israel.* Cambridge: Harvard University Press, 1973.

Moehring, H. R. "The *Acta pro Judaeis* in the *Antiquities* of Flavius Josephus: A Study in Hellenistic and Modern Apologetic Historiography," *Christianity, Judaism, and other Greco-Roman Cults. Vol. 3.* Festschrift for M. Smith, ed. J. Neusner (Leiden: Brill, 1975) 124-158.

Mölleken, W. "Geschichtsklitterung im 1. Makkabäerbuch (Wann wurde Alkimos Hoherpriester?)," *ZAW* 65 (1953) 205-228.

Momigliano, A. *Prime linee di storia della tradizione maccabaica.* Amsterdam: Hakkert, 1968 (rep. of ed. of Torino, 1931).

_____. "The Second Book of Maccabees," *Classical Philology* 70 (1975) 81-88.

_____. *Alien Wisdom: The limits of Hellenization.* Cambridge: Cambridge Univ. Press 1975.

_____. *Essays in Ancient and Modern Historiography.* Middletown, CT; Wesleyan University Press, 1977.

_____. "Greek Historiography," *History and Theory* 17 (1978) 1-28.

Moore, Carey A. *Daniel, Esther, and Jeremiah: The Additions.* AB 44. Garden City, NY: Doubleday, 1977.

Moore, G. Foot. *Judaism in the First Centuries of the Christian Era.* Cambridge: Harvard University Press 1966.

Moore, J. J. *The Manuscript Tradition of Polybius.* Cambridge: Cambridge Univ. Press, 1965.

Mørkholm, O. *Antiochus IV of Syria.* Classica et Medievalia. Dissertationes VIII. Copenhagen: Gyldendal, 1966.

Motzo, B. *Saggi di Storia e Letteratura Giudeo-ellenistica.* Florence: F. Le Monnier, 1925.

Mugler, C. "Remarques sur le second Livre des Maccabées. La Statistique des Mots et la question de l'auteur," *RHPR* 11 (1931) 419-423.

Nachtergael, G. *Les Galates en Grèce et les Sôtéria de Delphes. Recherches d'histoire et d'épigraphie hellénistique.* Mémoires de l'Académie royale de Belgique 63. Brussels: Palais des Académies, 1977.

Nestle, W. "Legenden vom Tod der Gottesverächter," *ARW* 33(1936) 246-269.

Nickelsburg, G. W. E. *Resurrection, Immortality, and Eternal Life in Intertestamental Judaism.* HTS 26. Cambridge: Harvard University Press, 1972.

Niese, B. "Kritik der beiden Makkabäerbucher nebst Beiträgen zur Geschichte der makkabäischen Erhebung," *Hermes* 35 (1900) 268-307; 453-527. (=*Kritik der beiden Makkäbaerbucher.* Berlin: Weidmann, 1900.)

Nissen, H. *Kritische Untersuchungen über die Quellen der vierten und fünften Dekade der Livius.* Berlin: Weidmann, 1863.

North, R. "Maccabean Sabbath Years," *Bib* 34 (1953) 501-515.

Ohly, K. "Die Stichometrie der Herkulanischen Rollen," *Archiv für Papyrusforschung 7* (1924) 190-220.

_____. *Stichometrische Untersuchungen.* Beiheft zum Zentralblatt für Bibliothekswesen 61 Leipzig: Harrassowitz, 1928.

Opelt, I. "Epitome," *RAC* 5.944-973.

Palm, J. *Über Sprache und Stil des Diodorus von Sizilien.* Lund: Gleerup, 1955.

Papanikolaou, A. D. *Zur Sprache Charitons.* Cologne: Universität zu Köln, 1963.

Pardee, D. "An Overview of Ancient Hebrew Epistolography," *JBL* 97 (1978) 321-346.

Pax, E. "Epiphanie," *RAC* 5.832-909.

Pearson, I. *The Local Historians of Attica.* Philological Monographs published by the American Philological Association 11. Philadelphia: American Philological Association, 1942.

Pédech, P. *La méthode historique de Polybe.* Paris: Société d'Édition "Les Belles Lettres," 1964.

Peter, H. *Wahrheit und Kunst, Geschichtsschreibung und Plagiat im klassischen Alterum.* Leipzig: Teubner, 1911.

Pfister, R. "Epiphanie," *PW*, Supplementband 4.277-323.

Plöger, O. "Die Feldzüge der Seleukiden gegen den Makkäbaer Judas," *ZDPV* 74 (1958) 158-188.

Pomtow, H. "Delphische Neufunde," *Klio* 14 (1914) 270-276.

von Rad, G. *Der heilige Krieg im alten Israel.* 5th ed. Göttingen: Vandenhoeck & Ruprecht, 1969.

Reese, J. M. *Hellenistic Influence on the Book of Wisdom and its Consequences.* AnBib 41. Rome: Pontifical Biblical Institute, 1970.

Reeve, M. D. "Hiatus in the Greek Novelists," *Classical Quarterly* 21 (1971) 514-539.

Renaud, B. "La Loi et les lois dans les livres des Maccabées," *RB* 68 (1961) 39-52.

Richnow, W. "Untersuchung zu Sprache und Stil des 2. Makkabäerbuches. Ein Beitrag zur hellenistischen Historiographie," unpublished PhD Dissertation, Göttingen, 1967.

Robert, L. *Études Anatoliennes. Recherches sur les Inscriptions Greques de l'Asie Mineure.* Etudes Orientales V. Paris: E. Boccard, 1937.

Rostowzew, M. "Ἐπιφάνειαι,"*Klio* 16 (1919-1920) 203-206.

Roussel, P. "Le miracle de Zeus Panamaros," *Bulletin de Correspondance hellénique* 55 (1931) 70-116.

Ruppert, L. *Der leidende Gerechte: eine motivgeschichtliche Untersuchung zum Alten Testament und zwischentestamentlichen Judentum.* Forschung zur Bibel 5. Würzburg: Katholisches Bibelwerk, 1972.

Rydbeck, L. *Fachprosa, vermeintliche Volkssprache und Neues Testament. Zur Beurteilung der sprachlichen Niveauunterschiede im nachklassischen Griechischen.* Studia Graeca Upsaliensia 5. Stockholm: Almquist & Wiksell, 1967.

Schaumberger, J. "Die neue Seleukiden-Liste BM 35603 und die makkabäische Chronologie," *Bib* 36 (1955) 423-435.

Scheller, P. *De hellenistica historiae conscribendae arte.* Leipzig: R. Noske, 1911.

Schunk, K. D. *Die Quellen des I. und II. Makkabäerbuches.* Halle: Niemeyer, 1954.

Schwarz, E. *Fünf Vorträge über den griechischen Roman.* 2nd ed. Berlin: de Gruyter, 1943.

———. "Berichte über die catilinarische Verschwörung," *Hermes* 32 (1897) 554-608.

Segré, M. "La più antica tradizione sull'invasione Gallica in Macedonia e in Grecia (280/79 a. Cr.)," *Historia* (Studi storici per l'Antichità Classica; Milan: Popolo d'Italia, 1927) 1, No. 4, 18-42.

Sherk, R. K. *Roman Documents from the Greek East. Senatus Consulta and Epistolae to the Age of Augustus.* Baltimore: Johns Hopkins Press, 1969.

Speyer, W. *Die literarische Fälschung im heidnischen und christlichen Altertum; ein Versuch ihrer Deutung.* Munich: Beck 1971.

Stemplinger, E. *Das Plagiat in der griechischen Literatur.* Leipzig: Berlin, 1912.

Stern, M. *Greek and Latin Authors on Jews and Judaism.* Vol. I. Jerusalem: Jerusalem Academic Press, 1974.

Stockholm, N. "Zur Überlieferung von Heliodor (2 Makk 3), Kuturnaḫḫunte, und anderen missglückten Tempelräubern," *ST* 22 (1968) 1-28.

Strasburger, H. *Die Wesensbestimmung der Geschichte durch die antike Geschichtsschreibung.* Wiesbaden: F. Steiner, 1966.

Strugnell, J. "The Angelic Liturgy at Qumran: 4 Q Serek Šîrôt ʿÔlat Haššabbāt," *International Organization for the Study of the Old Testament, 3rd Congress.* VTSup 7 (Leiden: Brill, 1960) 318-345.

Surkau, H. W. *Martyrien aus jüdischer und frühchristlicher Zeit.* Göttingen: Vandenhoeck & Ruprecht, 1938.

Tcherikover, V. *Hellenistic Civilisation and the Jews.* New York: Atheneum, 1970.

_____. "Jewish Apologetic Literature Reconsidered," *Eos* 48 (1956), Fasc. 3, 169-193.

Torrey, C. C. "Die Briefe 2 Makk 1:1-2:18," *ZAW* 20 (1900) 225-242.

_____. "The Letters Prefixed to Second Maccabees," *JAOS* 60 (1940) 119-150.

Ullman, B. L. "History and Tragedy," *TAPA* 73 (1942) 25-53.

Wacholder, B. Z. "The Letter from Judah Maccabee to Aristobulos: Is 2 Maccabees 1:10b-2:18 Authentic?" *HUCA* 49 (1978) 89-133.

Walbank, F. W. *A Historical commentary on Polybius.* Oxford: Clarendon, 1957.

_____. "History and Tragedy," *Historia* 9 (1960) 216-234/

_____. "ΦΙΛΙΠΠΟΣ ΤΡΑΓΩΙΔΟΥΜΕΝΟΣ: A Polybian Experiment," *JHS* 58 (1938) 55-68

_____. "Polemic in Polybius," *JRS* 52 (1962) 1-12.

_____. *Polybius.* Berkeley: Univ. of California Press, 1972.

_____. *Speeches in Greek Historians.* The J. L. Myers memorial lecture 3. Oxford: Blackwell 1965.

_____. "Tragic History," *Bulletin of the Institute of Classical Studies of the University c London* 2 (1955) 4-14.

Wehrli, F. "Die Geschichtsschreibung im Lichte der antiken Theorie," *EUMUSIA. Festgabe fr E. Howald* (Zurich: Rentsch, 1947) 54-71.

Wichmann, W. *Die Leidenstheologie. Eine Form der Leidensdeutung im Spätjudentum.* Stut gart: Kohlhammer, 1930.

von Moellendorff-Wilamowitz, U. "Asianismus and Atticismus," *Hermes* 35 (1900) 1-52.

Wilhelm, A. "Zu einigen Stellen der Bücher der Makkäbaer," *Anzeiger der Akademie der Wissenschaften in Wien.* Philosophisch-historische Klasse 74 (1937) 15-30.

Will, E. *Kallisthenes' Hellenika.* Königsberg: Hartung, 1939.

Wooten, C. "Le Développement du style asiatique pendant l'époque hellénistique." *Revue des Études Grecques* 88 (1975) 94-104.

Würthwein, E. *Die fünf Megilloth. Ruth, das Hohelied, Esther.* HAT 18/1. Tübingen: Mohr, 1969.

Zambelli, M. "La Composizione del secondo libro di Maccabei e la nuova cronologia di Antioco IV Epifane," *Miscellanea Greca e Romana* (Studi pubblicati dall'Istituto per la Storia Antica 16; Rome, 1965) 195-300.

Zegers, N. *Wesen und Ursprung der tragischen Geschichtsschreibung.* Cologne: Üniversität zu Köln, 1959.

INDEX